1st written by Coach Rich Walker in 1968 and co written by Coach Acie Earl in 2012 as 1st Edition.
Cover Design by Acie Earl
Venom Media Copyright 2nd edition 2022
Venom Media Copyright 2012

Printed in the United States
ISBN:

Introduction

First and foremost I want to thank God- Allah for bringing me to this point. Now that I am at age 52 I am writing this book. I never knew if I'd make it through. To not be a bad statistic in some way, a broke athlete, or job-less etc, but nevertheless I'm through it and here and ready to give parents and kids my best drills and insight to improve.

Secondly all the credit goes to my mentor and ex college asst. Coach Rich Walker who inspired me to write my part of this book and write more books in general. As coach Walker was the only coach who has helped me to be a man and father and better person. As most coaches and players and teachers I've had [not Professor Teague -lol] and people I knew back when I played only talked about when I played and nothing about future jobs or the future of myself and things to come. Coach Walker always talked about what I should do now and what the future was, now the future is now and Coach Walker is a great credit to that.

Third, my family, my kids, Kenya, Keonna, Kacie and Kareem, as they are the sole reason I keep pushing and hustling and fighting each day in this world. I hope to live and see them have kids of their own, and my brother Dorian.

Fourth, my Venom kids, Venom sports girls and Venom sports boys who taught me alot. I got upset with them and them from time to time but again they keep me going and we've had some very good special times. Thanks parents for help and support on this book, as every coaching and training sessions we've ever done has helped me in this book. I hope we do many more to come with many new kids at www.venomsportstraining.com

I'm so glad I never took a college or pro job as I know in my heart and brain that God wants me here with you all. I'm staying in the Iowa City area with you all to help build the game in Iowa. Enough with the sentimental stuff, let's get down to hoops.

Table of Contents

Basketballs Main Ingredients:

1-<u>Coach Walker's Defense</u>

I. Objective
- a. To prevent the opposition from playing the kind of game he wants to play.
- b. To maintain constant pressure on the opposition to force him into ill-timed moves.
- c. To demoralize the opposition.
- d. To win!

II. Importance
- a. Single most important phase of basketball.
- b. Tough part of the game; not the fun part. Toughness and aggressiveness is the key to successful defensive play. The defensive player must be alert to dive for loose balls, knock down passes, tie up the opponent who has the ball, rebound aggressively, and in general, beat the opponent to the punch.
- c. You can always tell the competitor by his defensive abilities and successes.
- d. Anybody can have an "off night" offensively, but never on defense. Your team will always stay in the game despite an off shooting night if you play defense.
- e. You must play defense, not watch it. Watchers pay their way into the game and sit in the stands.
- f. If you must loaf pay your way into the game; if you have to catch your breath do it on defense.
- g. Hustle is that intangible factor that makes a superior player out of an average one. Hustle with hands high.

III. Ingredients
- a. Pride
    - i. Develop the defensive attitude by always taking pride in your

    defensive assignment

    ii. Make up your mind to stick to YOUR MAN.

    iii. Keep repeating to yourself. "He is MY MAN and I will stop him."

b. Determination

    i. Takes will power and toughness to stick to YOUR MAN, especially if he is a scorer.

    ii. Determine to constantly improve your defense. Now… Today… Tomorrow may be too late.

    iii. You must be determined that YOUR MAN is not going to score. You are going to "stuff" him.

    iv. Be determined that you CAN, WILL, and MUST contain YOUR MAN. You are better than he is and you will prove this to him.

c. Concentration

    i. Concentrate on YOUR MAN. Study him. Check his strengths and weaknesses. Look for give-a ways such as bouncing the ball and "killing" himself, shooting and/or dribbling one way. Pick up those tell tale movements of the eyes, hips, feet, etc.

    ii. Good defense takes absolute concentration on what you are trying to do.

    iii. Shut out all thought except those concerning shutting off YOUR MAN.

    iv. Hustle…Fight…Talk it up…Be alert… Practice…Practice… Practice.

IV. Stance

a. Body

    i. Upper trunk bent forward at the waist at a forty-five degree angle.

    ii. Back remains fairly straight.

    iii. Rear end kept low for low center of gravity to maintain good body balance.

b. Legs and Feet

     i. Legs bent at the knees

     ii. Feet shoulder-width apart in a heel-to-toe alignment (staggered stance); heels are off the floor and weight is on the balls of the feet.

     iii. Feet movement by using the defensive shuffle (boxer's) –step, close, step; quick, choppy types of steps; feet do not touch.

     iv. Do not cross feet when guarding a man unless you have lost him (Shame!) completely and have to run to intercept hi. Take the shortest route. Do not trail behind him.

  c. Head and Eyes

     i. Eyes riveted on the mid-section of the man with the ball because it is the offensive player's least effective faking medium. When he is actually dribbling the ball, concentrate on the ball.

     ii. Chin-up.

  d. Arms and Hands

     i. Palms of hand up to **flick up at the ball**.

     ii. Fingers spread wide.

     iii. Ball hand held higher; other hand low and wide to deflect passes, to use as a feeler (for screens), and to keep body balance.

  e. Defensive stance difficult to maintain; daily attention must be given to develop the stamina necessary to playing this stance.

V. Voice

  a. Use your voice to make teammates aware of opportune situation. Yell:

     i. **Ball** when the ball is loose on the floor.

     ii. **Shoot** when YOUR MAN shoots.

     iii. **Screen Left**, etc when YOUR MAN screens to teammate left.

     iv. **Dead** when YOUR MAN has picked up his dribble

  b. Become familiar with your teammates voices.

  c. User your voice to help a teammate, such as pick up the loose man, take the dribbler, watch the man cutting, post man high, pick right, etc.

    d. Be a Talking Tom but not a Wise Willy; positive talk not negative nonsense.

VI. Playing the Man with the Ball

    a. Arms length away from the man with the ball before he has dribbled.

    b. Middle of the body should be aligned with the ball in an overplay position.

    c. Halt the advance of the man with the ball.

    d. Maintain pressure on him until he gets rid of the ball.

    e. Prevent him from taking a good shot; force him into bad passing situations.

    f. Be aware of defensive rebounding and block out when necessary. Do not turn your head when YOUR MAN shoots to follow the flight of the ball. Your responsibility is to maintain the inside position of YOUR MAN and box him out.

    g. Never let YOUR MAN drive baseline on you. Overplay him so that you are playing on his baseline leg. Keep your leg nearest the baseline rearward.

    h. Drive YOUR MAN to the sidelines until he reaches the foul line or foul line extended. From this foul line or foul line extended force him to the middle where you can get help.

    i. Do not stab or reach for the ball. Be a leach. If you play good defense, YOUR MAN will give the ball to you.

    j. Make a shooter shoot over your outstretched hands; give him a limited view of the hoop.

    k. When the dribbler picks up his dribble, close in tight and straight up with your hands close together and on the ball. Be prepared to take two or more steps back to prevent him from the "give-and-go" move once he has passed the ball. Make his cut go behind you.

    l. When defending against a definite shot, jump straight up, not in toward the shooter. Either make his shot go above your hands or **occasionally** crouch low and run right at his belly and at the last minute duck under and continue down the floor for a sucker pass and shot.

   m. Do not be a Jumping Jack. Stay on your feet when YOUR MAN takes a shot. Leave your feet only when you are certain the ball is to be shot.

   n. Take a slide step back when YOUR MAN fakes a shot and gives any fake with or without the ball. Do not reach or stab at the ball when he fakes.

   o. Any time there is a cross or screen switch using your hands to push off on the switch. No need to yell switch. Man who does not switch is at fault.

   p. Take the initiative away from the offense.

VII. Playing the Man without the Ball: Denial Position

   a. Purpose is to pressure the offensive man **one-pass from the ball** in order to prevent the penetrating pass.

   b. Body

      i. Bent at the waist; straight back; rear end low for low center of gravity.

      ii. Body turned slightly toward the ball to allow for peripheral vision.

   c. Eyes and Head

      i. Chin up.

      ii. Head slightly turned toward the man with the ball to allow peripheral vision to include both the man and the ball.

      iii. Keep the ball in sight at all times.

   d. Feet and Legs

      i. Inside leg forward; toe of foot aligned with crotch of offensive man without the ball.

      ii. Feet in a staggered stance with the toe of the forward foot pointing at the possible receiver.

      iii. Heel of back foot off floor slightly; rear leg spread wide and comfortably.

   e. Arms and Hands

      i. Inside arm is extended in front of the receiver; palm turned toward the man with the ball.

  ii. Outside arm is held low; back of hand toward the receiver and brushing his uniform to feel the man for movement.
 f. Movement back and forth is by means of the defensive or boxer's shuffle.
 g. When the offensive man breaks for the basket, as he approaches the foul line area, the defensive man should abandon the boxer's shuffle and open to the ball by pivoting on his rear foot to the ball. Hands are held high to discourage the pass. Remember the man without the ball should be made to cut behind the defensive man, especially the man cutting from the corner to the hoop.
 h. In this position you are between the man and the ball attempting to force the receiver away from his objective. Denial of the ball.
 i. Challenge the opponent's reception of passes at all times. Make him work to receive the ball.
 j. Be alert to intercept or deflect any pass which the defender feels he has a good chance of getting his hands on.

VIII. Playing the Man without the Ball: Helpside Position
 a. Each defensive player on the helpside (two or more passes away) is part of a TRIANGLE, the points of which are: his man, the ball, and himself.
 b. The BASE of the Triangle is a line drawn from his man to the ball; the APEX of the triangle is the defensive man. He forms this apex by moving away from his man toward the ball.
 c. The helpside defender must follow **four** basic rules in forming the triangle:
  i. He should never be more than one step or two off the base of the triangle or the "line of the ball" in order to force his man always to cut behind him.
  ii. He must be close enough to the ball to stop penetration by the use of the dribbler or the pass if he is in the backline. Distance away from his man depends upon the quickness of the defensive man.
  iii. The farther the ball is from your man, the further you can be from your man.

  iv. Using peripheral vision, you must be able to sight your man and the ball.

d. Be alert to intercept or deflect any pass which the defender feels he has a good chance of getting his hands on.

e. Be alert to pick up any open cutter or dribbler if he is advancing into scoring territory.

f. Make all cutters go behind you, especially the man cutting from the corner to the hoop.

g. Be alert for double-teaming situations.

IX. Special Skills

 a. Defensive Fake

  i. Resembles the fencer's thrust and parry in body movement

  ii. Fake a thrust for the ball (maintaining good body balance) with arm and leg, then retreat using the defensive shuffle.

  iii. Do not stab. Once in a while if the dribbler is very careless and keeps the dribble high, go for the ball but do not foul.

 b. Double-Up

  i. The two-on-one situation for the defensive team.

  ii. When you have the double team, close off the dribbling area by interlocking legs with your teammate; close in tight and straight up with hands close together and on the ball.

  iii. Generally speaking it is a good risk on the following situations:

   1. Pre-planned trapping situations.

   2. When the second defender can approach the man with the ball while he has his back turned.

   3. When there is a close lateral hand-off.

   4. When the offensive player with the ball is driving blindly into a second defender's position, especially if he is driving toward the corner and YOUR MAN stays.

   5. When YOUR MAN stays high and the ball goes low, you play the ball not the man.

   6. For c and d above the defensive man should use the

jump switch or up switch rather than the slide switch.

X. Guarding the Pivot Man
   a. Once the high pivot has received the ball, back off one step and make him go into the middle to shoot. Never allow him the baseline.
   b. Play the pivot so as to prevent him from receiving the ball:
      i. Low pivot – front him
      ii. Medium pivot – Denial position same side as ball
      iii. High pivot – About one step behind him
   c. Continually call out the pivot's position to your teammates.
   d. If double cutting off the pivot, allow room for your teammates to slide through and switch on the second man through only when both cutters cut through on the same side.
   e. When a guard is driven into the pivot, he should aim for the inside shoulder of the post man so that he can roll to the inside shoulder of the new man on the switch.
   f. Shut off the pivot when he attempts to come up or over to receive the ball. Do not let him have his position. Make him go to another position.
   g. Play in front of the pivot when he rolls to the hoop hoping to receive a pass from his teammate. Remember all cutters are forced to cut behind you.

XI. Defensive Rebounding
   a. Getting into Position
      i. Momentarily watch YOUR MAN after the shot. Be ready to follow in the direction that he rebounds. Ride him away from the basket (but not back).
      ii. Pivot (Front or Reverse) and place your body in his path.
      iii. Spread feet wide, arms and elbows up and out, backside lowered to keep center of gravity low and make yourself strong to prevent being pushed out of position. Keep the attacker on your back (sit in his lap) but do not foul by forcing him backwards. Remember the lower you are, the stronger you

are in this position.

    iv. Step to close any distance that you have from the attacker.

b. Moving to Get the Ball

    i. After the attacker has been taken off the boards or blocked out, look for the ball, sight it, time your jump, and use a maximum effort leap forward and toward the ball. Your jump should be high, wide and forceful.

    ii. Snatch the ball away from the basket at the top of the leap preferably with one hand behind and slightly under the ball; the other hand above the ball; fingers spread wide in a strong grip.

    iii. Timing is essential; the eagle spread is an important part of the leap.

c. Keeping the Ball Away from the Attacker

    i. Rebounder should dome down with legs well spread and with elbows extended out from the body for protection. Cover the ball with both arms, and pivot away.

    ii. Ball should be opposite the chest and protected with a semi- crouch resulting from the eagle spread.

d. Get-Away

    i. Practice turning in the air and getting the ball away to fast break receiver before coming down to the floor.

    ii. Against light pressure, look for the outlet pass toward the sidelines.

    iii. Against light pressure, dribble to open area from the attacker but only if the pass is impossible to make.

    iv. The quicker you get the ball away, the faster break opportunities will be available; passes should be crisp and sharp.

XII. Good Defensive Tips

a. Do not foul. A good defensive man who maintains his correct positions does not need to foul. A poor guard often fouls because his man gets ahead of him. It indicates that the defensive man is not giving his best efforts and that in most cases he is loafing.

b. If you have a jump ball with an opponent other than your own man, be sure to point out your opponent to the teammate who guards the man with whom you are jumping.

c. Never enter a game without knowing who YOUR MAN is. Never leave a game without letting your substitute know who YOUR MAN is.

d. Be sure to keep good defensive balance at all times. Always have one man beyond the top of the circle and a half-check man slightly lower than the foul line extended.

e. When guarding the man out of bounds, concentrate on the ball and not the man. Wave your arms vigorously. Make it difficult for the man to pass the ball inbounds.

f. Do not allow three point plays.

g. If you get caught in a two-on-one situation, stay in the middle of the lane. Use the defensive thrust to make the dribbler commit himself. Try to shut off the passing lane to the other man.

h. If you get caught in a three-on-one situation, use the same moves as in a two-on-one situation.

i. If you get caught in a three-on-two situation, line up in a tandem (one behind the other) with the lead man slightly above the free throw line and the second man halfway to the hoop. Lead man's duty is to stop the ball as high as possible and make the offense pass. The second or low man picks up the lead pass while the original high man drops low to the basket (again tandem) to shut off feed for a lay up to the third offensive man.

j. Good defensive work is 5% inspiration and 95% perspiration.

2-**<u>Coach Earl's Defense</u>**

Defense that is taught the old way is another misconception on what you need to be a good defender. Once again, you need to have the desire and will to play defense. Many coaches will teach stance, foot work, vision and some hand/eye coordination. Stance is overrated; of course, you have to be in some type of stance and which type of stance you use depends on what position you play: Guards need probably 80-90 %, forwards 50-60% and post players 10-20% of the time you need to be in a stance.

Guards- have to keep the opposing guards from going around them. Easier said than done as guards are usually the quickest players. They have to be in a stance and slide their feet or first off don't allow the offensive player to get the ball to drive in. Either way the player has to slide their feet and get down in a stance. The guard is expected to pester the opposing point guard up the floor and get a few poke aways from their guards. Also they need to be in a position to take a charge when it's time to come down and help out defending on the opposing team's best scorer. So to review, a guard has to be in a stance and use their feet about 90 + % of the time.

Forwards-have to play help side defense to help out when another teammate gets beat. They also have to guard the opposing team's best wing players. Again, they have to shuffle their feet and don't let the player get the ball. The big thing for defense of the wing players is to be aware of what is going on the weak side of the floor. Wings can not hug their player that they are guarding. Otherwise he or she will be out of position when the main action is going on the strong side of the floor. The wing is expected to block a few shots, grab any loose balls and take a charge every once in a while. This player should be in a stance about 70 % of the time. But I will warn that when a coach sees a wing player standing straight up, they think he's lazy. A wing player has to be at least in a stance most of the time.

Post Players- are expected to not allow the opposing post players score. It can be done in a lot of ways. You can front the player fully by getting your body in front of his body. Or he or she plays half way [denial] —which means to deny with 1 arm bar but leaving your feet behind or sideways to the player. Or they can play behind and try to alter or block the shot. When I played against Michigan State, against Mike Peplowski a big Polish 6-10 guy about 280 lbs, He'd allow the ball to come to me then body me up and alter my shot by physical tough play. It Didn't work, as I averaged 26pts vs. Michigan State, my highest point team avg in the Big Ten. Coaches often have different takes on how to guard the post. I was a shot blocker since the 3rd grade. I was coached by my dad until the 7th grade so he taught me how to block shots. He taught me to play behind the post and then I waited for them to shoot, then I'd block it. I would then block it to me or block it out of bounds, which ever had the best effect on the game/player. Some coaches forbid the ball to go into the post as they say it breaks down the defense so they want players to front the post. Some coaches tell the post defenders to change up depending on who they are playing. High level coaches always do this as they want the offense to dictate how the post is played.

Example: When I played against Luc Longley and Rony Sikley, I was taller than them and had longer arms. I could always block their shot or disrupt it, so I could play behind them. But when I played against David Robinson and Patrick Ewing I had to front or push them out as if they got the ball it was an automatic 2 points because they were so good and skilled players.

It's very likely a post player has to come out to guard a wing or guard at least 1 time a game and even now more since the game is changed. There is more pick and roll and the big guy has to switch out on the guard up top. In that case, they have to at least show a stance, maybe guard a smaller player or two for a short possession. I often say that if a defense player shows a strong stance then the offense player is more likely to fail to try to drive around them or even try. If a player plays straight up and down then an offensive player is more likely to test him. Think of it like this, if you see a police officer you slow down or try to fasten your seat belt. But when you don't see a cop you drive how you want.

Some great defenders over the years I've seen and/or played against.

1- **Shane Battier** was a great wing defender who used his body to take charges, was not quick and not very athletic, and he wore a size 17 shoe. He also was good at blocking shots even though he's only 6-7. I love the way he played, he was always in a stance, always trying to make the defensive play and guards the opposing team's best offensive player. He played at Duke Under the great K and you can see it in his defensive philosophy.

2-   **Nate Robinson** is an excellent guard defender. He was only 5-7 if that, but a great jumper that won the NBA dunk contest twice and playing college strong safety in the Pac 12 with Oregon or Oregon State. Nate was a pesky active defender who was a top 5 NBA league leader in steals and even blocks despite his size.

3-   **Bill Russell- was** a great post defender, and even the best NBA and college defender ever, might have been Bill Russell. He used his long arms and brain to trick defenders into bad shots and even blocked shots to himself versus out of bounds, or out of play. He was the mastermind behind not blocking every shot and not fouling. Bill blocked tons of shots but often tricked defenders into shooting bad shots as they thought he was going to block or foul them.

4 . **Hakeem Olajuwon** and **Tim Duncan** were also great post defenders despite not having a lot of bulk or superior strength. Both were position defenders and used timing and smartness to block shots at the end of games when the game counted most. Olajuwon also was a NBA leader in steals and blocks as he had cat quick reflexes after playing soccer as a youth. Duncan was a great swimmer as a youth that helped him use his great hand/foot coordination.

4-   **Alvin Robertson** was maybe my favorite defender ever. I played with Al with the Toronto Raptors. He was coming off back surgery and sat out a year or 2 before that season. When he played for the Milwaukee Bucks he once had a quadruple double in points, steals, rebounds and blocks. He was only 6-4 or 6-5 but could block shots and defend with anyone. He was big up top muscle wise and strong as an ox who also wrestled in high school. He once bet Oliver Miller he could take him down and pin him and they wrestled one time before practice in the locker room, for a few minutes until coaches came in. Big O was over 350 lbs I think at that time. Alvin would teach us all his tricks for defending, grabbing the jerseys, tapping the shooting arm, hitting the leg, head butting the guy out of position and using your head to push the guy back, riding the guy out of position, hand in the face, all the little knick knacks of defending. Al played in the 80's and 90s where only tough defenders succeeded. He had to guard Michael Jordan, Ron Harper, etc and even guarded Shaq one time when he was with the Detroit Pistons. The story was Shaq was a rookie and was going to set a record of most points by a rookie I think, and the Pistons big guys were fouling out and scared to guard him as Shaq was dunking all on them. With a few minutes to go in the game Shaq had 40+ points and the Pistons called a time out to go over a strategy to not let Shaq get the

record. They decided to grab and foul Shaq and none of the big guys wanted to do it, so Alvin said "I'll do it if y'all are scared". A real man of his word, as the Pistons came out of the timeout and Shaq was guarded by Alvin. Alvin was pulling him down, grabbing him, fouling Shaq intentionally and then Shaq got fed up and the 2 came to blows. It's a great YouTube moment to watch. In Toronto, our coach Brendon Malone called Alvin a true Raptor when it came to describing him at a press conference or a team dinner.

4-Ron Artest, maybe one of the 1st defenders who had strength and agility, as he was strong as a bull, but agile on his feet back in the day. He was smart and used his strength to beat you out of position. Everyone remembers him in the Detroit Pistons brawl but he was a great defender before and after that with the Knicks, Bulls and Lakers. He won NBA defensive player of the year a few times and even had a stat that he shut down more players when he was guarding him then other good defenders in the NBA.

5-   **Bruce Bowen**. A great success story indeed, he was un-drafted and played in the CBA with the Rockford Lightning, a CBA team I coached after he was there. In order for him to make an NBA team he had to learn how to defend great NBA players. He did all the dirty work for his teams and he was not fast, couldn't jump and not strong at all, but he won a few defensive player of the year awards in the CBA and NBA. He also had some stats where fewer players scored on him when he guarded him.

6-**Kobe Bryant**. He often wanted to be like **Jordan as we all know**. But in his quest to be like Jordan I think he surpassed Jordan. In my eyes I think he was better than Jordan. he defended better players and had greater offensive numbers. Just saying lol, I played against both.

Jordan was the standard yes, he started to play defense like **Jordan.** As good as Kobe was offensively he was defensively just as good. Kobe used his head, long arms and athletic ability to shoot the gaps and get steals, block shots and deny good players the ball. Like **Jordan**, Kobe will and has guarded the best players on the other team. He holds players accountable also for guarding their man as he led so by example.

7-   **Michael Jordan**, maybe one of the best all time defenders to ever play. He never took a night off defensively and took it upon himself to guard the best player. He blocked many center's shots and stole the ball from guards, came from the weak side for steals and traps. When the game was on the line he would deny the ball to the best player. He in essence taught a lot of players how to be the best scoring player and best defender.

8-   **Scottie Pippen... Jordan's** Robin to Batman. Both of them were a tag team duo offensively and defensively as well. Pippen was long and athletic and could jump so there wasn't anything he couldn't do and or guard. His long arms would poke away balls like he was Plasticman. He often guarded the point guard to keep the point guard out of the lane or to make plays.

9-LeBron James, as they say this guy can guard any position. His body style allows him to body up centers and his strength allows him to guard forwards and his quickness allows him to guard guards. His shot blocking ability to come from the weak side and chase the ball down on the fast break, you tube some of those blocks. At the time of this 1st edition of the book, LeBron was still in his prime, so we'll see how good of a defender he will end up being but even today he can be an elite defender.

To summarize defense is like rebounding, desire, heart, and sweat, and a little bit heady but a lot of feistiness. If you can do those things a coach will always want you on a team.

3-<u>Coach Earl's Zone Defense</u>

Zone defense- There are many types of zone defenses and the premise of some defenses is to guard an area or space, not a man to man. Tall athletic teams do well in zones and slow down non athletic teams. They also defend well in the zone as they don't have to move that much. The key to playing zone defense is still using man to man principles. Meaning you still have to defend your man and not let him shoot over you, dribble around you, or rebound over you. Zones are good to use against teams that don't shoot well, and or not coached well as the offense has to find a way to beat the zone. The zone is also used to protect players in foul trouble. Or to hide players, who can't guard well, or semi injured players or even teams that are tired from travel or multiple games like at AAU tourneys or NCAA tourney games, where teams play multiple games in a few days. If I see my teams are sluggish from the night before or dragging from a lot of games then I'll go to a zone for awhile or a game or two to rest them.

Types of Zones

A-2-3 is the most common zone with 2 small guys up top on each elbow, and the other forwards and center across the front rim with the big guy in the middle and forwards on each box. The 2-3 zone is as old as basketball itself. Back in the day most teams could not shoot well so it worked well against teams with only 1 or 2 good shooters.
B-3-2-, now more common as most teams can shoot better than the teams of yesterday. More big guys can shoot well, especially forwards like **Paul Gassol, Kevin Garnett, Rasheed Wallace, Karl Anthony Towns, Kevin Love, Anthony Davis and Nickola Jokich**. Back in the day only 1 or 2 players could shoot 3's so a 2-3 zone was effective. But now with post players and forwards shooting 3's , the 3-2 is a great zone to play to guard against the better shooters. At Iowa we played a 3-2 most times but it was different as the 3 man or the small forward was the guy in the middle up top. He also slid down and fronted the post when the ball was passed or dribbled to the corner. Then the 3 man slid back up to guard the perimeter. In my youth coaching, I often play the **3-2** to rest my players and keep my perimeter players guarding the 3 point line. When I coached at Solon high school I used it against teams that got hot against us from the 3 point line. But I never slid my 3 man down into the paint, all three of my perimeter players stayed around the 3 point line for less movement. The 2 big players stayed inside to guard the lane. With Coach Davis's 3-2 zone at Iowa the big

guys had to guard the corner. I'm a firm believer that the big players should stay close to the basket. But each coach is different and they have their own beliefs in what works. Coach K in man to man, Coach Boehiem in zone, both won over 1000 games, so who was right lol.

3- 1-3-1, often used as a gimmick defense , even back in the day as even Dr. Tom told us at Iowa.   He thought that the 1- 3- 1 is the worst defense to play, I believed that for years until I started coaching at Solon high school. When I took the head Solon boys freshmen job I met with Coach Randall at the high school. After we took the tour, we talked about paperwork. We sat down at the lunch table and he asked me what I thought about the 1-3-1. I said it was a bad zone to play and only teams that didn't know what they were doing used it.   He then drew it up and explained it to me and said his teams even went to state with it in the past. I was skeptical at first, but the way he drew it up, it made sense. As the year went on I watched more and more of it and our teams were very good at each level, frosh, soph, and varsity. That year our varsity team went to the sub-state game and lost. I still could not figure it out totally but I saw some things that intrigued me about it. Matter of fact when I played youth ball from the 3-6th grade my dad coached me and we used that type of zone. But, the way he coached it ,was the big guy[me] and was under the basket all the time and the best, most athletic player played the middle, the small scrappy kid hawked or chased the ball up top and pestered each pass, All over the court. The weakest kid always was the weak side wing and other good players on the strong side wing.

However, Coach Randall played the big guy in the middle and other big guy's weak side wing so he can drop down in the post when the ball is on the strong side wing and corner. The fastest-smallest kid plays under the basket then goes to the corner if the ball is passed or dribbled; there as he is a trap guy in each corner. Then the most athletic or longest kid is the top player to hawk the ball, but he never drops down below the free throw
line.

Coach Randall studied the 1-3-1 from a head coach from Metro State University in Denver along time ago. The coach won multiple championships at the D-2 level and then coached on George Karl's staff at the Denver Nuggets many years ago. The coach has verbal and hand signals calls for a trap up top which is called fire, and another call for trap down low for playing a good
post player. Example, black is the call for the trap in the corner, shadow is the call for following a 3 point shooter and sag is the call when the players sag off the perimeter and pay much detail to the best post players. I was amazed how this looked when it was drilled and explained well.

The key to the 1-3-1 is at youth and small time levels that it works well, for a few reasons:

A-Youth teams are small, and normally don't have alot of tall players. With the 1-3-1 the key to beat it is to pass over the top and lobs work well. In D-1 power 5 college, semi pro, overseas, NBA; those leagues/levels players are taller 6-9, or

7-footers, so it iss easy to pass over the top, ETC-At those levels, Point guards are normally around 6-6 like **Jason Kid**, and forwards are tall like Kobe, LeBron and they are 6-7 and 6-8. In youth or high school there are not extremely tall kids or kids who maybe can catch a lob dunk. In my 25 years plus of youth coaching AAU, semi pro, camps and high school, I've only had lobs dunked on to our teams twice ever.   The opposing team passed over our teams in the 1-3 -1 for a lob dunk. It was Mo Kan Spice as they had 5 to 7 D-1 players on their roster at an AAU Tourney in Kansas City, i had 2 at best even d-3 juco players.

B-The bottom line is teaching the 1-3-1 how you want to. My Venom and high school teams had rules and we stick by our rules and it works 99% of the time. It disrupts the other team's passing and we got stuck in some games versus better players /teams just because the other players couldn't pass or catch the ball. I played it with my daughter's AAu teams with Kenya under the basket, as she was often our tallest player, best rebounder and shot blocker. I had her to never leave the basket area to scare players. We've had some quick players to play the top. They had to just hawk the ball handlers as they couldn't bring the ball up versus us most of the time. The key is, most teams have to practice against it often to be effective. Especially in youth leagues, AAU teams or high school, ETC. Most teams barely practice 1 time a week, and if that at best. To put in 15 minutes a week to game plan versus us using the 1-3-1, with the game plan against us puts us at an advantage and the other team at a disadvantage.

That's why it works, plus most youth kids are bad passers, bad catchers and don't process information that well at younger ages. The coach might have a special zone offense for the 1-3 1, but the team will forget it or go back to their regular man to man offense, ETC. You don't know how many times at Solon I've witnessed the opposing team's quick time out and the coach screaming at the players on the supposed zone offense the coach wants them to execute or what they worked on in practice. Then we put that 1-3-1 back on them and they keep turning it over. Even in youth leagues versus our past Venom teams the coach is screaming like crazy. Then I know I had them, they as a team think the pass is open, when it's not. We go to steal the ball, most teams guard the ball, plus most teams see and play man to man, or 2-3 zone all the time, the 1- 3- 1 is different. Some coaches and teams don't even know what we're in until halftime or after the game is over.

Also kids do not shoot well at the younger ages, so you can leave a few kids wide open and or dare kids to shoot you out of the zone. In college or even high school kids some can knock down a wide open shot. But in the youth levels, they shoot it over the backboard or air balls mostly.

C-The last key to the 1-3-1 is to trap out of it and be aggressive. My teams played it aggressively and that is why it worked. We did not sit back and let the ball get passed around and or dribbled around. Teams and parents knew how we played it and refs knew we played it. I've gotten berated by parents and coaches and even refs leaving the gyms after games on how I supposedly got our kids to play too hard or aggressive at that level. I teach the kids not to reach and foul and the refs knew that. We've often played a half and not fouled or a whole game and only fouled 4 or 5 times which is unheard of for a team to press and trap all game /full court. Most kids would reach or be out of position and then foul, or be tired and foul. I subbed regularly and we have rules so we were never out of position. When our kids reach and get a foul, I often side with the Ref and tell the ref [good call] I never fouled when I played and I expect our players not to foul. Matter of fact I only fouled out of 2 games my whole college career. Once in my freshmen year and once in my senior year in college. I often tell coaches and parents a team is a direct reflection of its coach. If the coach is unorganized and flipity, the team runs no offense and is high in turnovers. If the coach is late to games the players are normally late and they don't get a good warm up. If a coach is an ex football player or wrestler then the team normally grabs, fouls and plays too physically.

4-1-2-2 zone, this is a glorified aggressive 3-2 but made popular by our Solon high school rival, former Mid Prairie coach Don Showalter. He then went on to coach varsity boys at Iowa City High School. By then he got hired by USA basketball to coach the 16u boys and has won many Olympic gold medals.

Typically teams haven't seen the 1-2-2 in years until you play against a unique team such as Mid Prairie HS back in Solon conference play. His top guy or the 1 would chase the ball and his other 2 short guys played the elbows and then both big guys on the boxes. It's played like the 2-3 where players kind of sit back and let the offense come to them, only the top guy is the most aggressive guy. But sometimes they trapped the corners out of it. Coach Showalter had calls to trap up top and corners, ETC. When I was a kid playing in tournaments I used to see this defense sometime but I don't see it too much anymore at youth levels but now in the NBA and college it is making a comeback to stop dribble penetration and good guards.

5-1-1-3, Is a real junk defense, played in a full court setting mostly. I've seen this zone in the Big West and Mountain West conferences in the last 2 or 3 years. The top guy hawks the ball; the other middle 1 player plays the middle, free throw line area and the other 3 guys, the forwards on the box and big guy under the basket. Some variations of it have the two top guys switch, so 1 top guy takes the 1st pass the next top guy takes the 2nd pass. Then the 1st guy replaces the other guy and switches off so 1 guy is always covering the middle free throw line area at all times. It looks very wild and crazy but sometimes works against teams with not good players.

6-Triangle and 2, the 2 tall players are on the boxes and the most athletic player by the free throw line. The other 2 guards, or 1 guard and 1 forward are chasing and denying the other team's best 2 players when they get the ball. This works in youth league and or high school as most teams at that level have only 1 or 2 good players and the other players are role players/ stiffs. A few years ago when I coached high school, opposing teams did that with our Solon varsity teams. Teams also did it against us to stop our all state players, **Ben Weeks,Matty Gleason** and, **Matt Morrison;** who went to play at the University of Northern Iowa. They tried to stop us and slow us down. We've even used it a few times and even with our Venom teams at the AAU tourneys to slow good players down like some of the 12 plus D-1 players I coached back then.

My old coaching plan was to hope the opposing teams have not game planned against it. That only happened only a few times where the coach just took his best player out since he had no offense to run versus the junk defenses.

7-Box and 1- is the most common defense to stop one good player. Your best player now will guard the other team's best player man to man. Or you can put your worst player to play their best player to just waste a player on them. The other tall players are on each box, while the two small players are on the elbows. Both the triangle and 2 and box and 1 are betting the other players can't beat you. You stop the best player and dare the other offensive players to beat you. You are betting the other players are trying to find their best players to score like their normal offensive sets. If your defensive players can key in on those passes to them then they can anticipate and maybe try to steal the ball.

8-6-1, born out of the 1-3-1 is another junk defense I learned. There is no top guy, as the top 1 player now plays the best player 1 on 1. The other 4 players are still playing the 1-3-1 in their areas. The middle player now has the hardest responsibility as they have to play the middle free throw line area and the top 3 point area. It is a hard guard if the other team has a good Shooter from the top. It is basically a zone with 4 guys and 1 guy man to man with a 1-3-1 shell.

9- 7-2, Again born out of the 1-3-1 as a crazy junk defense. It's called 7-2 in my old Solon team's era. In my 2nd and 3rd year of coaching at Solon, I finally found out what coach Randall was talking about when he'd scream out, we should go 7-2. I'd nod my head and say sure, lol. With the defense 7-2- it means actually 2 guys playing man to man by taking the top guy and the middle guy out of the 1- 3- 1 or the top and bottom guy. We've used it many times at the Solon varsity level to win games. The great thing about it is the other guys are still playing 1- 3- 1 rules so it does not change your other players' defensive duties.

To sum it up, zones are tricky, and every zone has a purpose, or it should. Some teams and players can pick zones apart and others do well and find the seams, creases or open areas. Carmelo Anthony and Lebron were great like that. The key is to find out which zone your team plays well and what zone they don't. If you run into a rut or dead end with the zone, get better at it or get out of it. I'll never forget the year at Solon when we won the State Championship. We were in a dog fight at Dewitt in a conference game. At halftime the score was 10-12. They were shredding our 1-3-1 and Coach Randall went man to man for 3 or 4 plays in the 3rd quarter and then we went back to 1-3-1, and that was the key. In my 5 years at Solon I've never seen Coach Randall play man to man, but he did that year and realized sometimes you have to get out of a zone.

All these types of defenses have their place in the game, at the lower the level and now at the higher levels. With the younger players, age, less experience and coaching, the more the junk defenses work better. With the older and more experienced teams, you had better have good coaches so the defenses are harder to beat.

I once watched a college game, Butler versus Loyola Chicago. My old buddy Rodell Davis,who I played with at Iowa, who hosted me on my recruiting visit, was recently an assistant coach at Loyola University in Chicago. They were changing defenses every play down, 2-3, 1-3-1 and man to man to junk up the game and confuse Butler. And the other defenses were working somewhat but Butler had 2 tall guys and they were throwing over the top of the 1-3 -1 each time to beat it. My point was great coaches and great players can break down any defense, if you give them time and preparation. Loyola back then just would not get out of it. They lost big time as they had to guard Butler's big guys when they got it down low off of lob passes. Again if you're going to play junk defenses then play it hard, play it aggressively, and play it smart.

Great man to man teams were the University of Illinois, in the Fighting Illini era. George Karl's Seattle SuperSonics with **Shawn Kemp**, Gary Payton and **Sam Perkin, Detlef Schrempf**. They switched everything on defense. Bob Knight's University of Indiana teams were good as well, and University of Duke's teams are always very solid along with the Coach Tarkanian UNLV teams.

Great 2-3 teams were Syracuse with Derrick Coleman. North Carolina with **MJ, James Worthy, Sam Perkins**, and **Kenny Smith**. Also Temple with **Don Chaney had** created a matchup zone that many coaches copied and still use today.

Great 1-2-2 teams, were Georgetown, Louisville under Coach **Denny**

Crumb with Pervis Ellison and my best NBA friend of all time Greg Minor. Minnesota also played a little of that against us when I was at Iowa with coach
Clem Haskins another famous trapping and pressing coach.

Great 1-3-1-teams, were the Lakers, when the subs came in, in the show time era, normally in the 2nd quarter. Our Solon teams were great also. In one State tournament game the opposing didn't score a single point in the first quarter, which is still a state record. Our Venom AAU teams learned to be great at it. We would often shut down teams that average 30-40 points a game and hold them down to 10-15 points in games. We once won a game in the 6th grade 50-5. We had to tell our players in the end don't always steal the ball. Sometimes I had to put in some of our 3rd 4th graders as subs to not run the score up versus the other teams.

6-1 Zone Defense

1-3-1 Zone Defense

1-2-2 Zone Defense

1-3-1 Zone Defense

2-1-2 Zone Defense

2-3 Zone with high trap at half court

Box and 1

Triangle and 2

Venom Players practicing defense

<u>Coach Walker's Ball Handling</u>

I. Dribbling
   a. Probably the most abused of the basketball fundamentals.
   b. When dribbling you should have a purpose in mind. Too many youngsters dribble with no purpose other than dribbling itself and an unwillingness to give up the ball.
   c. Four basic objectives or purposes of the dribble are:
      1. To advance the ball when you cannot pass.
      2. To drive for a score or through a defensive opening.
      3. To escape from a pressing defensive player.
      4. To set up an offensive series or option.
   d. In order to be an effective dribbler or ball handler you must be able to dribble with **both** hands effectively.
   e. Types of dribbling to master include:
      i. Basic Dribble
         1. Control
         2. Speed
      ii. Change of Pace or Stutter Dribble
      iii. Change of Directions or Cross Over – Switch Dribble
      iv. Reverse or Spin Dribble
   f. In order to be an effective dribbler you must also be able to pivot right and pivot left while dribbling.
   g. Starting Position of the Dribble
      i. Head and Eyes
         1. Keep your chin up so that you can see your open cutters and teammates
         2. Do not look down at the ball; keep your eyes focused up court. You will have slight visual contact with the ball through the use of peripheral vision.
      ii. Body
         1. Your body should be bent at the waist or in a semi- flexed (crouched) position so that you actually are

leaning into the ball. This will give you better ball control and speed.

2. Your shoulder opposite the dribbling hand is slightly forward.
3. Your abdomen is in.
4. Keep your body between the ball and the opponent when necessary.

iii. Legs and Feet

1. Legs are bent at the knees and one foot is in front of the other in a staggered stance.
2. Keep your weight evenly distributed on the balls of your feet.

iv. Arm, Wrist, and Hand

1. Upper arm is forward so that the elbow is in front of the waist and away from your body; upper forearm is parallel to the floor.
2. Lower arm is forward and parallel to the floor; it is kept in a bent position to discourage the defensive player from trying to steal the ball.
3. Wrist is in a semi-locked position.
4. Fingers are spread comfortably; your hand is cupped to conform to the ball. Remember you control the ball with your fingertips; never use the palms of your hand.

h. The Action of the Dribble

i. The action of the forearm, wrist and hand is that of a pumping or pushing motion.
ii. The hand pumps in a downward motion about three or four inches and remains there until the ball comes back to meet the fingertips. You are actually pushing or gliding the ball to the floor by use of your fingertips with the wrist and slight forearm movement. Do not slap or strike the ball to the floor.
iii. When the ball rebounds from the floor into the fingertips, both the ball and the hand should "ride upward" for about three or four inches.

iv. The ball should strike the floor to the right of your foot
(when dribbling right-handed) and slightly forward foot. For
left- handed dribblers, the ball should strike the floor to the
left of your left foot and slightly forward of the forward
foot.

v. Keep in mind that the speed of your dribble should be
determined by how well you control the ball at that rate
of speed.

i. Basic Variations of the Dribble

  i. Change of Direction – Cross Over or Switch Dribble

1. Used to outmaneuver an overplaying defensive
player and to change directions quickly.

2. The dribbler should plant his inside foot (the foot
opposite the dribbling hand) hard, pivot slightly and
push off that foot in the direction that you now wish to
go. As you are pushing off the inside foot, your
forward foot crosses over your body in a long stride in
the direction you wish to go.

3. As the dribbler changes direction he changes his
dribble hand by dribbling the ball across and close to
his body to the opposite hand.

4. When transferring the ball to the other hand make
certain that your hand is on the top right (if changing
directions to the left) or the top left (if changing
directions to the right) of the ball and not under the
ball.

  ii. Reverse or Spin Dribble

1. Used to outmaneuver a severe overplay on the part of
the defensive man.

2. Should be used with extreme care and an awareness
of the defensive players. Many defensive teams use
this move to double-up on the dribbler.

3. While dribbling the offensive man makes a reverse
pivot off his inside foot (foot opposite dribbling hand)
changing his dribble to the opposite hand while
making this move.

4. Keep the ball close to your body and put your body

between the ball and the defensive man as you are changing hands.

5. Make the exchange of hands on the top side part of the ball, not under the ball.

iii. Change of Pace or Stutter Dribble

1. Used to outmaneuver the defensive man into leaning forward toward you and possible making a lunge at the ball. In any case by shifting his weight forward or toward the ball, this should give the dribbler an opportunity to drive (burst) by the defensive man.

2. Dribbler while using a basic dribble comes up to his defensive man.

3. As he approaches his man he slows his dribble and for a very brief moment actually stops moving forward.

4. At this exact moment he shifts his weight from his forward foot to his rear foot and quickly back to his forward foot while at the same time giving his defensive man a head and shoulder fake.

5. This faking or rocking or stutter moment is followed by a quick burst of speed forward on the part of the dribbler.

j. Good Dribbling Tips

i. Be especially wary when catching a pass with your back towards your own basket and immediately start to dribble without first looking to see if there is a defensive man on your back waiting for you to charge him or waiting to steal the first dribble.

ii. Remember once you have used your dribble you can be tied up by the defensive man because you cannot go anywhere.

iii. Develop a variety of fakes or feints before you start your dribble (See section on Pivoting and Offensive Footwork).

1. Various types of cross over steps

2. Rocker step

3. Head and eye fakes

iv. Basically use a belt high or slightly higher dribble for the speed dribble and keep the ball below the waist for a control dribble. How low you keep the ball is determined by the defensive man's coverage. The important thing to remember is that you should dribble to the height that is comfortable to you and one that you can control.

    v. Do not try to dribble through a mass of players. Stop, pivot and pass the ball to a teammate.

    vi. Do not wait for practice time to learn how to dribble. Work at home and at every opportunity to improve your skill.

    vii. Learn to dribble and pass off the dribble.

    viii. When picking up your dribble, stop with your feet parallel to allow you to establish either foot as your pivot foot. When practicing dribbling practice coming to a stop with your feet parallel.

II. Passing

    a. The pass is the most effective manner of advancing the ball.

    b. The passer's ability to advance the ball is enhanced if he can utilize a variety of passes. Remember you cannot use the same pass in all situations. Different situations call for different types of passes. A good passer should include in his repertoire:

        i. The Chest Pass

        ii. The Two-Handed Bounce Pass

        iii. The Two-Handed Overhead Pass

        iv. The Baseball Pass

        v. The One-Handed Bounce Pass

        vi. The Hook Pass

    c. Passes should be made by using many of the same fundamentals used in shooting:

        i. Fingertip control

        ii. Use of the wrists

        iii. Follow through

        iv. Good body control and a comfortable center of gravity

    d. Peripheral vision is very important in good passing and ball control.

      i. Know **where** your teammates are and **what** they are doing at all times.

      ii. Know **where** the defensive men are and **what** they are doing at all times.

      iii. This is done by seeing out of the corner of your eyes and like any basketball skill takes constant practice to perfect. You can and you must be proficient in this too often neglected skill.

e. Most passes should have a backspin on the ball.

f. The Chest Pass

      i. The chest pass is probably the most frequently used pass (along with the bounce pass) in the game of basketball and mastery of this pass is a necessity to anyone who wishes to play the game. It is used in the short passing game.

      ii. Starting Position: Head and Eyes

            1. Chin up

            2. For beginners the eyes should be concentrated on the target area which is the chest area of the receiver. Once you have mastered this type of pass, the use of peripheral vision will allow you not to telegraph the pass but the target remains the same – the chest.

      iii. Starting Position: Body

            1. Semi-flexed position

            2. The body is slightly bent forward at the waist for balance

      iv. Starting Position: Legs and Feet

            1. Feet are placed slightly apart one in front of the other in a staggered stance in a heel to toe alignment.

            2. For a right handed passer, the left foot forward; for a left handed passer, the right foot forward. When stepping forward with the pass, step with your forward foot.

      v. Starting Position: Hands, Fingers, Elbows

            1. The hands are placed on the sides of the ball with control of the ball by your fingertips (never use the palm of your hand to touch the ball) comfortably spread to

conform to the ball.

2. Thumbs are on the back of the ball and pointing at each other.

3. Elbows are close to the body but not touching the body and are in a bent position.

vi. The Release of the Chest Pass

1. The ball is held directly in front of the body chest high with the fingertips of both hands.

2. Release the ball with a straight arm extension thrusting the arms forward using both wrist and finger action while stepping toward the receiver with your forward foot. This step will give you good follow through of the arms and body in the completion of the pass.

3. The release should be a strong snapping action which is applied by extending the wrists with an inward snap of the thumbs, spinning the ball off your fingertips.

4. Remember to aim for the chest area of the receiver.

5. After releasing the ball your arms should be fully extended in a follow through (you can actually feel your elbows lock). The palms of your hands will be then facing the side line area slightly and be facing the flight of the ball and your thumbs will be facing each other or pointing to each other.

6. Once you have mastered this skill you will be able to snap the ball quickly without the full extension of the arms or the step forward.

7. As the pass is released the passer's rear foot should be on the ball of the foot not flat on the floor.

g. The Bounce Pass: Two-Handed

i. This pass is used when there is a defensive man between the passer and a teammate to whom he is passing. Also the small man working against the big man can use this pass effectively. When a direct pass can be made, however, the bounce pass should not be used.

ii. This pass is used in the short passing game.

iii. The starting position of this pass is the same as that of the chest pass except that the ball is held in a position between the waist and the chest (comfort dictating), and the eyes are focused (for beginners) on a spot on the floor where you want the ball to strike which is about two-thirds of the distance between the passer and the receiver.

iv. The release is an outward and downward thrust with finger and wrist snap. At the release note that the palms of your hands will be facing the floor.

v. Take care not to put backspin on the ball other than the normal spin caused by the snap of the fingers and wrist. A bouncing ball is difficult to catch with a strong backspin or any spin.

vi. Note that the pass should come to the receiver in the area between his knees and hip or waist.

vii. This pass, like the chest pass, may be started with both feet parallel or with your feet staggered in a heel to toe position. Whichever is more comfortable to you, you should use. The point to remember is that you should step forward with the pass for body control.

h. Two-Handed Overhead Pass

i. This pass is very effective for taller players and a good pass to feed the pivot or a cutter.

ii. Body position is erect.

iii. Carry the ball above the head with both hand – one hand on each side of the ball and slightly on top with the thumbs in back. Ball should be slightly in front of the head.

iv. Extend the arms approximately three-quarters length to take full advantage of the passer's height. Elbows slightly bent and out.

v. Release the ball with a forward and downward thrust of the arms.

vi. Use sharp downward finger and wrist snap when releasing the ball with the thumbs following through in a downward position. Finger and wrist snap is downward and slightly in. When the ball leaves the hands the palms are facing the floor and fingers are pointing down.

i. One-Hand Bounce Pass

i. Should not be attempted until the two-hand passes
are mastered.

ii. More deceptive than the two-hand bounce pass but is used
in the same situations.

iii. Body position in a semi-crouch.

iv. Feet in a staggered stance, left foot forward when passing
with right hand and right foot forward when passing with
the left hand.

v. Carry the ball with both hands, one on the back and the
other on the front of the ball to a position near the tip. Right
hand passes will use left hand on front of ball and right hand
on the back; left hand passers vice-versa. Fingertip control.

vi. Remove the hand from the front of the ball as the
pass is started.

vii. Sing the arm forward and downward bouncing the ball on
the floor. The ball should hit the floor about two-thirds of the
distance between the passer and the receiver.

viii. Retain good body balance and follow through by
bringing the back foot forward in stride. Remember to step
toward the receiver with the front foot as the ball is being
released.

ix. The pass should be received in an area between the knee
and the hip.

x. Do not put any extra backspin on the ball other than the
normal backspin caused by the snap of the finger and wrist. j.
The Baseball Pass

i. Should not be attempted until the two-handed passes
are mastered.

ii. The baseball pass is used by the passer who is open or
loosely guard to an open teammate down court;
especially useful in the fast break game.

iii. Body position is erect.

iv. Feet in a staggered stance with left leg forward for
right- handers and right leg forward for lefthanders.

v. Ball held chest high with both hands on the ball. Inside hand (hand opposite throwing hand) on the front of the ball to the bottom side for control purposes; throwing hand in back of the ball. Fingertip control, well spread comfortably to conform to the ball. Ball should be held low enough to allow the passer to see over.

vi.   Carry the ball above the shoulder to a position behind the ear dropping your inside arm and hand for balance and shifting your weight rearward while carrying the ball further back with the throwing hand for good leverage.

vii. Note that the inside hand is swung down and out for balance.

viii.   Throwing arm is swung forward in a straight overhead throw close to the side of the head (no sidearm or sideward snap under any circumstances). A sidearm motion will tend to have the ball curve and you want a straight throw.

ix. Ball is released with full arm action letting the ball leave the hand over the fingertips of the fingers straight through the ball with a slight backspin.

x. Shoulder and arm follow through fully.

xi.   Upon releasing the ball the rear foot will slide forward in stride with the pass to retain good body balance.

xii.   At the conclusion of the pass fingers are straight and facing downward, palm facing the floor.

xiii.   Do not use peripheral vision; stare the ball into the receiver's hand. When you use this pass the cutter down court should be free, hence no need for peripheral vision.

k. The Hook Pass

i. Effective pass to start the fast break from a rebound. Also effective when the offensive man finds himself crowded to the sideline or corners.

ii. Ball is held in both hands; inside hand on the bottom front of the ball for control purposes; shooting hand directly behind the ball. Fingertip control. Fingers spread comfortably to conform to ball.

iii. Ball is held approximately waist high and brought slightly toward the body before taking the long take-off step.

iv. Body in a semi-crouched position, bent slightly at the waist and knees.

v. As the ball is brought upward the passer takes a long step forward with his inside foot firmly planting it while bending his knees for good body balance and control; weight shifts to the inside leg. Passers will use this inside foot to pivot and as a take-off to get into the air.

vi. The pivot and take-off step should be made on the ball of your inside forward foot.

vii. Jump above the defensive man with the inside side of your body toward the receiver.

viii. Face the receiver by turning the body in the air as soon as your feet leave the floor. Eyes focused on the receiver.

ix. As the step is started, the arms are fully extended and will begin to move upward in a smooth, sweeping motion. Both hands remain on the ball until the shooting hand moves directly under the ball and takes over completely. The inside arm continues to move into position that will help to protect the ball from the defensive man.

x. Ball is carried into a passing position above and behind the head and shoulder.

xi. The pass is delivered with a forward and downward swing of the arm and sharp finger and wrist snap, the ball leaving the hand after full arm extension over the tips of the fingers in a backward motion (backspin).

xii. As the ball leaves the fingertips, the wrist should be snapped for proper release.

xiii. Pass should be received shoulder high.

xiv. After releasing the ball the arm should have a complete follow through swinging naturally to the side of the body.

xv. Passer should come down lightly on his toes, feel parallel, body bent at the knees and waist in a well balanced position to move quickly in any direction.

l. Good Passing Tips

     i. It is important to control the ball once the defense has secured it. Treat the basketball as if it were 20-karat gold.

     ii. Vary your passes utilizing all passing planes.

     iii. Master feints and fakes which will prevent interceptions. Do not telegraph or unknowingly let your opponent know where and when you are going to pass.

     iv. Watch your teammates and pass away from his defensive man.

     v. Be extremely careful in passing the ball laterally across the court at any time.

     vi. Keep two hands on the ball so you can pass, dribble, or shoot.

     vii. Pass to a point somewhere between the waist and chest; to a man in motion give a lead suitable to his speed.

     viii. Learn to pass while on the move and to a man on the move.

     ix. Follow through on all passes for accuracy and good body balance.

     x. In receiving a pass, go to meet the ball. Be where you **ain't**.

     xi. Do not jump in the air to pass. You may find the man you intended to pass to, covered by his defensive man with you in the air and no place to go and no one to pass to.

III. Receiving the Ball

   a. Anytime a basketball is thrown, it must be caught. Yet catching is one of the least practiced skills. Many turnovers are a result of poor receiving techniques rather than passing mistakes.

   b. There are three basic principles to keep in mind when catching a basketball:

     i. Concentration on the Ball.

       1. Master visual concentration by focusing your eyes on the ball.

       2. Follow the flight of the ball from the time it leaves the passer's hands until it reaches you. Look the ball into your hands.

     ii. Arm, Hand and Leg Readiness

1. The receiver should always reach for the ball; it may be only a step or a forward leaning motion but you go to meet the ball not wait for the ball to come to find you. In this way you can prevent a possible interception and discourage your defensive man from trying to steal the pass.
2. The elbows should be bent and the arms extended with the fingers spread comfortably. The thumbs will be closer to each other than the fingertips of each hand.
3. Legs are bent slightly at the knees; body in a semi-crouched position to allow you to adjust quickly to a high or low pass.

iii. Catching the Ball

1. Always catch the ball firmly with two hands and use only your fingertips; never use the palms of your hand to catch a basketball.
2. When the ball strikes your fingertips develop the habit of allowing your arms to give with the ball, the distance depending upon the force of the pass. You do this by flexing both arms inward toward your body drawing the ball toward the chest in one motion.
3. If closely guarded by the defensive man bring the ball in close to your lower chest area to protect it from being taken away from you.
4. Remember to stare the ball into your hands. When you have to bring the ball into the lower chest area as in (3) such an action will result in a slightly spread of the elbows which will help protect the ball.

c. Good Receiving Tips

i. Never take a pass for granted. Just because the ball is large it does not mean that it is easily caught. Remember you have a defensive man who is trying to prevent you from receiving the pass.

ii. Only as a last resort should a player reach for the ball with one hand.

iii. In catching a low pass, you should bend a little lower and turn the palms up so that the little fingers are almost touching.

iv. In catching a high pass a receiver should turn his thumbs together while his palms open to the ball. Reach forward for the ball when possible so that there will be some give to the catch. Raise your head to see the ball.

IV. Jump Balls

a. Although the number of jump balls varies in games, controlling the tap can make the difference between winning and losing a close game.

b. Special exercises such as knee bends, jump roping, and tapping the ball up against the backboard again and again without permitting it to come to rest in the hands will aid in jumping ability.

c. Techniques used in jump ball situations.

i. Once you enter the jump ball circle, get set immediately and concentrate on the ball. Keep your eyes on the ball until after your fingers have directed the tap to a receiver.

ii. Right hander's should turn their right shoulder to the opponent in the jumping circle; left hander's, their left shoulder. Same foot should be extended.

iii. The forward leg is extended about the width of the shoulders. Knees are bent. The forward foot must be in the smaller center circle.

iv. Bring only the tapping arm up; the other arm should be kept low because you can raise your shoulder higher with one arm and therefore will have a higher reach.

v. Keep your chest and shoulder forward in the preliminary jumping motion. Do not bend backwards.

vi. The jump must be slightly forward and up since the ball is thrown up directly between the two men. However, do not jump forward too much so as to cause contact with the other man.

vii. Carefully study the officials' methods of tossing the ball to determine proper timing. Timing is vital and leaping too early or too late means the loss of the tap. Plan your leap so that you will leave the floor just before the ball reaches its maximum height. Remember you cannot tap the ball before the ball has reached its highest point.

viii. Control the ball on the tips of the fingers on all short and medium taps. Tap high and to the outside of the intended receiver. Do not slap it. If you try to slap the tap you will lose valuable height.

ix. Be prepared to tap the ball a second time should the first tap be deflected. However, remember that you cannot tap a ball more than twice unless another player other than the jumper touches the ball. You cannot tap the ball with two hands nor can you catch the ball.

x. Alight from the jump ready for action either defensively or offensively. You cannot leave the jumping circle until the ball has been tapped.

d. Good Jump Ball Tips

i. If your team uses signals to determine a play, be sure that you have the signal before you move into the jumping circle.

ii. If you are being out jumped consistently, politely ask the official to throw the ball higher. This is purely a psychological move. The change in height might cause your opponent's
timing to be off but if it doesn't do not give up and concede any tap.

iii. Non-jumpers are not to enter the circle until the ball has been touched by one of the non-jumpers. The jump ball and jump ball restrictions end when the tapped ball touches one of the eight non-jumpers.

iv. To secure the tap, step in between the opponent and snatch the ball aggressively with two hands.

v. Never allow two opponents to stand side by side along a circle.

vi. Make certain in the opponent's front court your tallest men line up nearest the goal for defensive purposes.

vii. If you have a jump ball with an opponent other than your own man, be sure to point out your opponent to the teammate who guards the man with whom you are jumping.

viii.   When the official is ready to make the toss, a non-jumper may not move onto the circle or change positions around the circle until the ball has left the officials hand.

ix. . A jumper is not required by rules to jump and attempt to tap the ball but if neither jumper taps the ball, it is tossed again with both jumpers being ordered to jump.

Coach Earl's Ball handling

I'm going to separate ball handling into dribbling and ball handling, as both are different. First we'll talk about ball handling.

Ball handling is the skill of handling the ball with and without pressure from defense. How do you catch, shoot or dribble the ball and how the ball is held in your hands and how it feels with your fingers. When the ball gets tipped or comes to you, do you bobble it or catch it cleanly in your hands? Do you as the player always come up with loose balls or make great plays with the ball? Some players have bad hands as they say mostly because they don't work on their ball handling skills and drills.

Some kids, parents and coaches think a player has great hands naturally. Of course it is not true; like all skills, it has to be honed and/or drilled. When Talking to older coaches and teachers, most agree that back in grade/middle school; more of the older Physical Education skills were linked to ball handling later in life. Games often played such as Dodgeball, Jacks, Kickball, 4 square, and Volleyball were (just to name a few) played. All were great games that made kids catch and throw a ball in gym class all year-round and taught hand eye coordination. The great thing was all kinds of balls and sizes were used so a player was taught how to handle all kinds of balls in their hands. These taught children the importance of holding the ball correctly or hand-eye coordination, which is extremely important in many competitive sports.

These days, P.E. classes aren't the same, many games are not being played or played competitively at all to not make kids feel bad or have low self esteem.

I feel as Trainers and coaches, we now have to go back and teach the old school ball handling drills in practice more than in years past. I once went to the Final Four in Tampa 2008 when **Candace Parker** from University of Tennessee won the National Championship. Stanford was there as one of the Final 4 teams. Before they had practice, the players all had a ball and formed a small circle at half court. The seniors were in the middle and they went through a 15 minute quick ball handling routine, trying to not drop the ball. Matter of fact, the whole routine is designed to not drop the ball and the only sound we should hear were the balls slapping against their hands. I remember I don't think anyone dropped the ball from Stanford.

For ball handling we separate it into ballhanding with the dribble and without the dribble.

Some great ball handling drills to teach/use with no dribble are?

1.   **Ball Slaps**- player slaps the ball from one hand to the other as hard as they can. It should be loud and used as a warm up to wake up the hands and fingers.

2.   **Rain Drops or Pitty Pats**- The player places the ball in the middle of their hands and flips it quickly between the two hands. It should be quick so the ball does not rest in the palms or with both hands together. Only the finger tips of your hand should touch the ball. When this happens you hear a raindrop sound. Pit pit pit pat pat pat should be the sounds you hear.

3.   **Body Circles or Around the World**- When the players pass the ball around their stomach and back as fast as they can. Then reverse it, then around their head and around their knees, and then ankles. Then the ball of going from head to stomach to knees and back up.   Of course as fast as the player can move it without the ball touching the floor.

4.   **Figure 8**- or pretzel, the player passes the ball between your legs from front to back making a pretzel or figure 8, then reverse the action.

5 . **Single leg circles**-Where the ball gets passed around the knees and the ankles, on each leg separately.

6.   **Front Back Flips**-The player bends down in a squat position and then flips the ball from the back of their body to the front of your feet as fast as the player can flip it without the ball hitting the ground. The ball starts and stays in between their legs.

7.   **Pretzel Flips**-same stance; instead of two hands in the front and on the back of the ball. One hand is in front the other on the back of your body between your legs like a spider. The player flips the ball and then switches the hands alternating from front to back of their body. The player tries to not let the ball hit the floor.

8.   **Figure 8 shuffle**-The player passes the ball in the figure 8 pretzel position. Then the player shuffles his feet with one foot in front of the other as the same time the player passes the ball between their legs in a figure 8 position.

9.   **Pretzel shuffle**-The ball is flipped and hands switched as the player shuffles their feet front to back in a figure 8 motion.

10. **Figure 8 walk**-where the player does the figure 8 while walking forward,

or walking backward. From half court or free throw line to the baseline and back.

11-**Pretzel shuffle walk**-Where the player shuffles and walks forward or backward while doing the pretzel flip.

There are some drills to practice dribbling stationary in place:

A-**Right hand power dribble**- The Player pounds the ball as fast they can with right hand and finger tips to control the ball. The other hand guards the ball with an arm bar out in front of their body.

B- **Left hand power dribble**-same action above with left hand.

C-**Push-pull**, right hand, then left hand. The ball is dribbled on the side of their foot and hand movement is like testing bath water, back and forth.

D-**Right left cross over**,-Ball is dribbled to left side and right side of body, as toes face the basket.

E-**Dribble dribble cross** - cross switch , cross cross switch ,or dribble dribble cross - you dribble twice with same hand then switch hands then dribble twice with that hand and then switch.

F-**Dribble dribble thru**- 1 leg is up and 1 back and the ball is dribbled on the side of the body, dribble dribble then thru the legs.

G-**Dribble dribble back**, -Both feet are parallel and pointing to hoop and you dribble the ball in back of your body [back].

H-**Dribble figure 8**- player stands in basketball stance, wide and dribbles the ball in between 1 leg then the other in a pretzel motion, then reverse.

I--**Right hand on right leg-as left the hand dribbles thru left leg**, then reverse. Player only dribbles through 1 leg as the other hand is on the other knee. Then the player reverses motion on the same leg then switches sides/hands.

j-**2 hand ball bounces**- The player passes the ball in between both legs with both hands on the ball. Then with both hands catch the ball, as hard and fast as they can.

k-**Spider dribble**- 2 hands touch the ball in the front of your legs but not together at the same time.   Then both hands dribble twice in front then the back.   2 dribbles in the front, then 2 dribbles in the back. When it gets fast, it looks like the player has multiple hands going on at the same time as the Ball stays in the middle of the body in between the legs.

L-**Walking spider**- You'd do the same drill but walk forward, my daughter **Kenya Earl** invented this when she was in the 4-or 5th grade. Then another kid I trained, Nick **Lindeman** from North Scott, invented it going backward when he was 5-6th grade. Another kid I trained, Jordan **Garrow** from Davenport North High School tried for years to invent 2 ball spider but couldn't get it, but he was close.

M-**dribble walking figure 8**- Dribble dribble then crosses thru legs then use other hands and do the same thing.   The key
is the left hand dribbles thru the right leg and vice versa, also a player can do it backwards.

N-**Dribble dribble step up walks,** same motion as you dribble 2 times with 1 hand then step up with opposite leg then push the ball thru or cross over. Then switch the action to do the same motion with the other hand. You can also do it backwards.

As I stated above, many coaches, trainers, and parents don't teach these drills anymore. They don't believe in their importance as parents just want their children to be able to just dribble fancy and shoot. Plus the players don't like to do them anymore and work hard to improve.   Most think that practicing them is boring and not fun. As a trainer and coach, I strongly believe in them and teach them even to my own kids. I believe it helps them handle the ball so that they can become more comfortable.   It helps their left-right side brain coordination to develop better. It also helps in limiting turnovers and miss-handles. We also do them with fancy balls such as dribble pro balls endorsed by **Lisa Leslie** from the **WNBA.** The ball has rubber knobs on them so it never bounces the same way each time.   Big balls which are oversized balls that look like a big kick ball. They are twice the size of a normal ball and hard to handle. Even dribble goggles that are worn as plastic blinders under the eye to make sure players can't look down at the ball. Those things help to make our players handle the ball better and are online for sale.

Some players had good hands and often had a knack for ball and never turned the ball over:

1-   **Oliver Miller**-often broke dexterity records with the Toronto Raptors. He'd make plays with the ball that left you wondering how he did it as he was 6-9 and 300 lbs plus.

2-   **Danny Manning**-a big forward who handled the ball and passed with ease, labeled as point forward when he played college and pro

3-   **Scottie Pippen**- again the ball was like an instrument in his hands, some say a grapefruit as he often ran the offense in close games with the Chicago bulls

4-   **Goose Tatum** from **Harlem Globetrotters**- he did many ball handling drills and invented many more that are still used today. He handled the ball like a magician, all on his finger tips. Goose did the tricks with the ball, and his teammate **Marcus Hanes** was maybe the best dribbler in the world at the time, Marcus taught **Curley Neal** and all those guys might be in the Guinness Book of world records at 1 time and great globetrotter greats.

5-   **Brian Garner** and **Kevin Smith** from the University of Iowa both had cry handles as we'd say on the street but made poor decision with the ball after the great move. But both handled the ball with ease; maybe the best in Iowa basketball history.

Figure 8 Dribble

Figure 8 with no Dribble

Figure 8 Shuffle

Figure 8 Reverse no Dribble

Rain Drop-Pitty Pat by the Chest

Pitty-Pat Over the Head

Left hand push pull

Left Leg Circles

Dribble Dribble Cross

Left Hand Dribble Around Left Leg

Coach Walker's Shooting

I. General Consideration of Shooting
   a. Body Position
      i. Proper Control of the body and body balance is critical for accurate shooting.
      ii. To shoot off-balance means that you are either a "hungry" player or that you have given up; the shot is generally a poor one and poor shots lose games.
      iii. Square your shoulders, hips and feet to the basket before shooting.
      iv. Hips are dropped to help the body lift and aid the wrists, fingers, etc. in propelling the shot. This center of gravity should not be too low nor too high but in a comfortable position to produce a smooth, flowing motion. Knees are dropped with accompanying bend to aid in the action of the shot. Body is slightly forward.
      v. Feet are placed flat on the floor at the start of the shot and are comfortably spread approximately shoulder width to give the shooter a firm base for the body. A shot properly executed comes as much off the tips of the toes as off the tips of the fingers.
      vi. Shoulders are relaxed and loose and are allowed to drop slightly.
   b. Concentration
      i. Relax and concentrate. Single most important part of making the shot is concentration.
      ii. You should concentrate on the target area before, during, and after the shot but the peak concentration should come the instant before the release of te ball.
      iii. Concentrate on a small target area on the shooting surface - sight the basket. For beginners the best target area would be a point just over the front rim; the advanced shooter may find concentration on the middle of the back rim more suitable to his needs. While shooter you should be concentrating on this

point and have a mental image of the area in your mind. Sight on the shooting area and be consistent on the sighting area.

    iv. Do not follow the flight of the ball. You should actually see the ball twice: the first time as it breaks the plane of your eyes
before the release and the second time as it breaks the plane of your eyes as it is coming down through the hoop.

c. Confidence in Yourself is key.

d. Take the high Percentage Shot when you can.

    i. Statistics prove that the team getting and making most layups will win. It is not always the number of shots, but the best percentage that wins.

    ii. Best percentage shots in the best order are below:

        1. Lay up

        2. Down the lane from the foul line in

        3. Top of the circle

        4. Side shot opposite the foul line

        5. Corner shot

    iii. Work for and take the best percentage shot. Do not take the second best if the best is available.

e. The Shot as a Whole

    i. Must be smooth with no jerking or snapping motions.

    ii. Ball must be held firmly but gently on the fingertips and pressure from thumbs must be avoided. Fingers well spread.

    iii. Spin the ball using a natural spin (reverse).

    iv. Ball is released off the V created by the positioning of the fingers and thumb.

    v. Ball must be made with a sufficient arc (medium arc) 6 – 8 inches above the hoop.

    vi. Follow through is an important part of the sequence of the actual shot.

    vii. Shot should start from the toes, knees, shoulders, arms, wrists, and fingers but the shot is controlled by the wrist and fingers.

II. Types of Shots

    a. The Layup Shot

        i. The shooter softly lays the ball up against the backboard a few inches above the rim so that it falls through the net.

        ii. Basketball's simplest shot yet it is missed too many times primarily as a result of the failure to observe the basic fundamentals and as a result of a lack of concentration.

        iii. Adjust the stride so that the feet hit the floor on a one-two count for the take-off step to the shot.

        iv. Take-off step is at a high jump angle lifting your knee high and straight up toward the basket. You raise the same knee as the shoot hand. Do not take your take-off step at a broad jump angle as this type of step will cause you to bang the ball off the backboard too forcefully thereby causing the ball to carom off the rim or away from the rim. Poor body balance also results from this type of take-off step.

        v. The take-off step to the basket must be made on the ball of the foot opposite the shooting hand. This foot must be firmly planted before executing your jump.

        vi. Ball is carried above the head with both hands in preparation for the shot. For the overhead layup shot the shooting hand is behind the ball slightly to the shooting hand side with the back of the hand facing the shooter while the support hand is under the ball slightly to the support hand side of the ball. For the underhand layup shot the shooting hand is under the ball slightly to the shooting hand side with the back of the hand facing downward while the support hand is at the top of the ball slightly to the support hand side.

        vii. Just before the ball is released, your support hand should be removed.

        viii. Release the ball off the fingertips softly without an intentional spin.

        ix. Make certain to jump as high as possible releasing the ball at the height of the jump and arm extension.

        x. On the release of the ball in the overhand layup shot the palms of your shooting hand should be facing the backboard; on the underhand layup shot the palm of your shooting hand should be facing the shooter.

xi.   The underhand layup shot is especially effective when shooting a layup at full speed because it is a softer shot.

xii.   All layups should be played off the backboards from the side. Focus about eight inches above and slightly in front of the rim (side); your eyes should be focused on this point on the backboard. If you must come head on for a layup, lay the ball just over the front rim.

xiii.   It is a good idea to get into the habit of looking back into the middle just before your take-off step (when the defensive man is on you) to see if one of your teammates may be open for an unmolested shot.

xiv.   Shot must be mastered from all angles; from the right side, the left side, down the middle, along the baseline in front of and behind the basket (past the basket is meant). Practice layups while dribbling from all angles and at various speeds;
receive the pass and lay the ball in; have a defense man on you to hinder (but not block) the shot. In other words simulate
game conditions as much as possible.

b. The One-Hand Push Shot

i. Eyes concentrating on the target area. Sight over the ball.

ii. Feet in a staggered, heel-to-toe alignment. Foot on the same side as the shooting hand is forward. Feet spread comfortably approximately shoulder width apart. Forward toe pointing to the basket while the toe of the rear foot is pointing away from the basket at approximately a 45 degree angle from the forward foot. Weight is even distributed for balance.

iii. Knees comfortably flexed; the further the shot the deeper the bend for maximum force from the legs.

iv. Shoulders are squared to the basket with the back straight. Waist is bent slightly and hips lowered so that the body has good balance; semi-crouch position.

v. Head should be in the middle and directly between the feet.

vi. Ball is held close to the body prior to the shot and somewhere between the shoulder and the eyes in front of the head to allow the ball to be sighted. Elbows are in close to the body.

vii. Shooting hand is directly behind the ball and across the seams of the ball; fingertip control; fingers spread in a natural, relaxed manner resulting in a well balancing positioning of the thumb and fingers to form the V position (extremely important since the shot will come off this position); index finger is aligned with the eye and the basket; palm of your hand off the ball.

viii. Supporting hand to the side of the bottom front of the ball for balance. Again fingertip control and comfortable spread of fingers.

ix. With knees flexed the shot should start from the toes and work up through the knees, shoulders, arms, wrists and fingers but the shot is controlled by the extension of the arms, the wrist, and the fingers.

x. Ball is released or shot off the V using fingers and wrist to control the ball.

xi. At the start of the shot, the shooter will dip the ball slightly. As the ball is started upward, the elbow moves under the ball. Note that the ball will be coming upward and backward.

xii. As the ball in the shooting hand moves backward the wrist cocks, the elbow should be completely under the ball and in front of it; the upper arm is now parallel to the floor while the forearm is perpendicular to the floor.

xiii. As the ball in the shooting hand starts forward toward the basket, the elbow unlocks and the wrist uncocks. There is a straightening of the knees as the shooter rises from the balls of his feet.

xiv. As the shooting arm extends forward toward the basket the ball should roll off the fingertips in a backward motion to create the backspin which produces the soft touch. Note that it is not pushed toward the basket with a stiff wrist action. The ball should be shot with a medium arc some six to eight inches above the basket.

xv.Hand and fingers then move under the ball and downward in proper follow through.

xvi.   Use proper follow through (should be able to feel your elbow lock when arm is fully extended) with arm fully extended; index finger should be pointing to the basket and your knees should be straight. Ball leaves the index and middle fingers last.

xvii. Important to use the legs and body so that the arm and wrist do not have to furnish all the power necessary to get the shot
to the basket. When the force behind the shot is generated from the legs and body, the arms are extended in a relaxed manner and the elbow and wrist snap merely accents the momentum started in the legs.

xviii. Peak concentration comes just prior to the release of the ball.

c. The One-Hand Jump Shot

i. Eyes concentrating on the target area.

ii. Shoulders squared to the basket. Back straight. Waist bent and hips lowered slightly so that the body angle is slightly forward for good balance. Semi-crouch position of the body.

iii. Head should be in the middle and directly between the feet.

iv. Knees comfortably bent; the degree of flex depends on the amount of force necessary for the jump. The further the shot, the deeper the bend.

v. Start the jump shot with feet parallel and spread the width of the shoulders. Weight evenly distributed.

vi.   Ball position is relatively close to the body somewhere between the shoulders and the eyes (shooter sights over the ball). The height of the ball depends on the distance from the basket or the force necessary to get the ball to the basket; the closer to the basket the higher the ball can be positioned to allow for a quicker release.

vii. Carry the ball up to position keeping it close to the body.

viii.   Shooting hand is comfortably spread and is directly behind the ball and across the seams of the ball; fingertip control;

fingertips spread in a natural, relaxed manner resulting in a balanced positioning of the thumb and the fingers to form the V position. Index finger is aligned with the eye and the basket.

The support hand is on the bottom front of the ball. Again fingertip control and comfortable spread of fingers. Elbows are close to the body.

ix. Jump straight up off the balls of the feet with full extension of legs, ankles, and feet. You should land in approximately the same position that you started your jump slightly forward of the jump-off position. Land lightly on the toes, feet parallel, body bent at knees and waist in a well balanced position to move quickly in either direction.

x. With knees flexed the shot should start from the toes and work up through the extension of the arms, the wrist, and the fingers.

xi. Ball is released or shot off the V using fingers and wrist to control the ball.

xii. At the start of the shot, the shooter will dip the ball slightly. As the ball is started upward, the elbow moves under the ball. Note that the ball will be coming upward and backward.

xiii. As the ball in the shooting hand moves backward the wrist cocks, the elbow should be completely under the ball and in front of it. Upper arm is now parallel to the floor while the forearm is perpendicular to the floor.

xiv. As the ball in the shooting hand starts forward toward the basket, the elbow unlocks and the wrist uncocks. There is a straightening of the knees as the shooter rises from the balls of his feet.

xv. As the shooting arm extends forward toward the basket the ball should roll off the fingertips in a backward motion to create the backspin which produces the soft touch. Note that it is not pushed toward the basket with a stiff wrist action. The ball should be shot with a medium arc some six to eight inches above the basket.

xvi. Release the ball at the summit of the jump for coordination. There should be a split second hesitation at the peak of the jump prior to shooting the ball to allow the shooter to reach

his peak concentration level at the release; then follow through to allow complete use of the body momentum. Hand and fingers then move under the ball and downward in proper follow through.

xvii. Use a complete follow through (should be able to feel elbows locked when arm fully extended) with full arm extension; index finger should be pointing to the basket and your knees should be straight. Ball leaves the index and middle fingers last.

xviii. Important to use the legs and body so that the arm and wrist do not have to furnish all the power necessary to get the shot
to the basket. When the force behind the shot is generated from the legs and body, the arm is extended in a relaxed manner and the elbow and wrist snap merely accents the momentum
started in the legs.

xix. When taking the shot at the end of the dribble, the dribbler should break his drive by planting his inside or leading foot and quickly square off into the correct jumping position **facing** the basket.

d. The Two-Hand Set Shot

i. Eyes concentrating on the target area.

ii. Shoulders squared to the basket; waist bent slightly forward and hips lowered for good body balance. Back straight. Semi- crouch position of the body.

iii. Head should be in the middle and directly between the feet.

iv. Feet should be parallel approximately shoulder width apart, toes pointing to the basket. Weight evenly distributed.

v. Knees comfortably flexed. The longer the shot, the deeper the bend.

vi. Elbows comfortably in, close to the body and slightly wider than the body in a relaxed manner.

vii. Ball is held with both hands on the sides (slightly to the back) of the ball; fingertip control; fingers well spread and comfortable across the seams of the ball; hands parallel with the thumbs diagonally inward toward the middle. Grip is firm but gentle. Do not squeeze the ball and put no added pressure on the ball with the thumbs.

viii.   Ball is held between the waist and the shoulder (preferably chest high) approximately eight to ten inches in front of the face. Sighting should be directly over the ball.

ix. Start the shot by bending the knees further while dipping the ball slightly downward and backward.

x. As the ball in the shooter's hands start forward to the basket, the ball is swung upward, extending the arms. The shot starts from the toes working through the knees, shoulders, arms, and fingers.

xi. Release the ball approximately eye level over the fingertips with an outward rotation of the wrists allowing the thumbs to roll through the ball causing the backspin which results in a soft shot.

xii.   Follow through with arms fully extended toward the basket; eyes on the target area; hands spread apart approximately the width of the ball with thumbs and fingers pointing outward and the palms facing the basket. Knees and body straight.

xiii.   Allow arms to fall naturally to place at the sides of the body; good body balance and be prepared to move in either direction.

e. The Hook Shot

i. Because the shooter must take a step and pivot before releasing the ball and will be holding the ball behind his body, footwork and stance is critical in executing this difficult shot which is also one of the most difficult to block.

ii. Shooter will most often receive the ball with his back to the basket. His feet are parallel, shoulder width apart. Weight evenly distributed.

iii. Head and shoulder fake should precede the long step and pivot prior to the shot. At the start of this pivot step, the shooter ducks his inside shoulder and firmly plants his inside foot by bending his knee to produce good body balance and control. This pivot step should be towards the basket for beginners. This will give you good rebound positioning. (See V)

iv. Ball should be held in a comfortable position approximately waist high and brought slightly inward toward the body before taking the long pivot step. Ball is held in both hands with his inside hand on the lower front of the ball towards the inside hand side of the ball; the shooting hand behind the ball slightly to the top; fingertip control; fingers spread comfortably.

v. As the ball is brought upward the shooter takes the long pivot step forward with the inside foot. At the start of this pivot step the shooter ducks his inside shoulder and firmly plants his inside foot by bending his knee to produce good body balance and control. Remember the step should be toward the basket. This forward foot will be used to pivot and to jump into the air. The pivot and take-off step will be from the ball of your inside foot.

vi.   Jump above the defensive man with the inside part of your body toward the defensive man to protect the ball. Face the basket by turning the body in the air as soon as your feet leave the floor. Eyes concentrating on the target area. Since most hook shots are taken from the side, the target area most often is a spot on the backboard approximately eight inches higher than the rim and slightly in front of the side rim.

vii.   As the step is started, the arms are fully extended and will begin to move upward in a smooth, sweeping motion. Both hands remain on the ball until the shooting hand moves under the ball and takes over completely. Inside arm continues to move into position that will help protect the ball. This arm position should be high and out in a bent position.

viii.   Ball is carried into the shooting position above and behind the head and shooting arm shoulder.

ix. Shot is taken with a forward and downward swing of the arm. The ball is released when the shooting arm almost reaches its highest position. The release is guided by the wrists and fingertips.

x. Ball should roll off the fingertips in a backward motion to provide the necessary backspin for a soft shot. As the ball leaves the fingers, the wrist should be snapped for proper release. After the ball is released the shoulder opposite the shooting hand should be pointing toward the basket; the shooting arm should fall smoothly and naturally to the side of the body.

    xi.   Remember since the shooting hand is almost completely under the ball, it is necessary to lift the ball in a little higher arc than most shots, especially if the shot is taken from in front of the basket and the backboard is not used.

    xii.   Shooter must come down lightly on his toes; feet parallel; body bent at the knees and waist in a well balanced body position to be able to move quickly and strongly for the offensive boards if the shot is missed.

III. Tips and Good Shooting

    a. It is best to practice the shots you will get in your offense:

        i. Front court men

            1. Shooting from the sides

            2. Jump shots from different spots on the floor

            3. Layups, especially along the baseline

        ii. Pivot men

            1. Hook and push shots

            2. Short jump shots along the lane area

            3. Layups and tip-ins

            4. Offensive rebound layups

        iii. Guards

            1. Two-hand and One-hand set shots

            2. Jump shots from foul line extended to top of key

            3. Driving layups

            4. Side shots below foul line extended

    b. Have a defensive man on you with his hand up when you shoot to hinder the shot but not block it.

    c. To learn to fake to set up your shots

        i. Head, shoulder, feet, and eye fakes.

ii. Ball fakes

iii. Rocker step

d. Use the backboards on short shots from the side. Most shooters do not use the backboards enough.

e. Foul Shooting

i. A good foul shooter must have a relaxed mind and body:

1. Do not step to the free throw line until the referee has the ball ready to hand to the shooter.

2. Take a deep breath and exhale just before shooting.

3. Bounce the ball

4. Shake your tightness off

ii. Intent concentration on the target area throughout the shot.

iii. Use basic fundamentals of the shot as explained in previous sections. Most common foul shot is the one-hand push shot. See section of this booklet devoted to this shot for proper techniques.

iv. Have complete confidence in your ability to put all your foul shots in.

v. When practicing your foul shots, do not be glued to one position. This is a false situation. Step off the line after every shot, or every other shot. Practice foul shooting when you are tired at times.

vi. Develop a rhythm to your shooting.

vii. To become a good foul shooter takes a great deal of daily practice.

f. Learn to shoot with both hands.

IV. Offensive Rebounding

a. Extremely difficult and takes a great deal of concentration and determination.

b. Be aggressive. Hit the boards hard.

c. Anticipate the shot and its possible rebound area and attempt to get into the inside position ahead of the defense. Remember field goal shots from the right side percentage wise go to the left side if missed and vice versa.

d. Evade block outs by maneuvering around the defensive man, spinning, rolling, or knifing around him. If you cannot get around him and in front of him, at least get in a position next to him but not behind him.

e. Hustle to get in second, third or fourth efforts.

f. Use two hands, snatch the ball, bring it down and depending upon the defensive man either pump fake and jump the ball in or aggressively go up immediately and jump the ball in. Vary your methods so that the defensive men cannot "get a book on you" and anticipate your moves.

g. If you cannot grab the rebound with your hands, attempt to tip it in (using the backboard when possible) with one hand or **keep the ball alive** by tipping it to keep the ball in play until you or one of your teammates can gain control of the ball.

h. Always but always time your jumps and jump as high as possible.

<u>Coach Earl's Shooting</u>

Shooting is an under rated skill that percentages show has been going down year by year since the 80's. When I grew up, a lot of kids could shoot as the game was not an athletic game yet; the game was not played above the rim yet. Back then there was no cable television so people didn't hear about **Darrell Griffith** aka "*Dr. Dunkenstein*" or **Dr. J** or **Spencer Haywood** ECT. Coaches stressed fundamentals and the skills as basketball hoops outside in the driveways were popping up all over America as kids shot outside. The kids who had the baskets were great shooters and all the coaches' kids were great shooters. Camps and clinics stressed follow through, shot pocket, seams and stance, elbow in ECT. Almost every kid knew how to shoot the right way.

The era of basketball from 1960 to 1980 had many great shooters; now as you fast forward to the modern day. Most kids and players can't shoot. The best players are high flyers, most of the high fliers developed jump shots later in their careers after they slowed down or experienced injuries, such as **Dominique Wilkins** when I played with him on the Boston Celtics. Dominique's nickname was the Human Highlight reel as his dunks were fierce. He tore his Achilles tendon around 1991 as the Atlanta Hawks traded him to the Los Angeles Clippers. While rehabbing he'd shoot over 1000 3 point shooters per day as he couldn't move around. When I played with him with the Celtics Dominique would shoot 2-5 3 pointers per game and it would surprise the defense even us as we all expected him to try to drive in and dunk all the time.

Here is a list of guys who added shooting to their game:

A - **Kobe Bryant** came into the league as young spry rookie oozing talent and dazzled us with his fast break dunks and super athletic finishes. As years went by his often comparisons to Michael Jordan kept coming and he saw to develop his jump shot was his way to show how his game has improved and score outside the paint as Shaq often clogged the lane with his 2 and 3 defenders.

B - **Tracy McGrady** was a young Kobe in the making as he scored so easy. He had a jump shot already when he came into the league and his constant injuries forced him to rely on the 3 point shot more and more where towards the end of his career he was only known for his 3point shot.

C -**Vince Carter** might have been the last great superstar we saw to add the 3 point shot due to battling injuries and slow decline of his game. With Vince his 3 point shot seems to rev up his game where he plays much better when he's hitting the trifecta's.

D - **Magic Johnson** and **Michael Jordan** were better shooters in the later part of their career as they added the 3 to their game.

As I teach shooting to my own kids and at clinics, I always tell kids and parents if you can get 1 or 2 of the 5 or 6 of the components of shooting that's great. Don't get bent out of shape if your kid's shot is not all perfect. What has to happen is that they perfect their shots by repetition. **Larry Bird** shot behind his head, Magic shot a push shot by his chest, **Michael Cooper** shot a 2 hand push, **Purvis Short** shot on the way down, **Bob McAdoo** shot behind his head and on the way down. **Kevin Martin** shoots a hitch shot that he kind of rolls off the side of his hip, **Nate Robinson** shoots at the apex of his jump as high as he can jump. **Jamal Wilkes** shot a spiral corkscrew behind his head and **Reggie Miller** banged both hands together after the release.

The moral of the story is that they were all good, above average, or even great shooters. But the key was that they all worked on the shot countless hours. As I learned a saying from Coach **Bruce Pearle** while working the Tennessee men's basketball camp a few summers ago, as he said to the campers, [Practice doesn't make perfect – Practice makes permanent] what he meant by that was it doesn't matter if you do it right or wrong but if you do it wrong you can perfect it or vice versa. So when it comes to shooting, the above players all practiced their own unique shooting form even though it has quirks or is fundamentally wrong.

My daughter Kenya was an 8th grader at the time of this 1st edition book. She was the tallest player we had on our Venom girls AAU teams. She was also our best shooter back in the day unitl better guards came like the Jonens girls who played at Iowa state, Illinois and Oklahoma. Two things I hammered home with her were [seams] and getting the ball up into a shot position above her eyes. The seams make it a perfect rotation shot every time and getting the ball up ensures she's aiming her shot. Most young kids throw the ball as they would a softball or darts. Kenya was a great shooter for her age and height because of the hard work in the gym and the values of her shot I instilled in her since the 4th grade. When she was a 3rd grader she shot a push shot, with 2 hands.   She was not strong enough to shoot correctly as our team played on a 10 foot basket in league play. She was our best player and we needed her to score and shoot to win games. As a parent and trainer, I was cringing every time I let her shoot that way.   But as coach I needed her to shoot anyway she could for us to win. I told her and myself I would change her form in the summer after league play as she was growing and getting taller. It was hard for her and me as she was used to making shots the push way. As I got a hoop in our driveway the first thing I did was lower it to about 9 feet and only let her shoot around the basket. Most parents make the mistake to let their kid shoot anyway they can if they make it and let their kids shoot on any size hoop and any distance. Each month I raised the basket as she got better at shooting, which allowed her to keep her form correct.

The last component of shooting is where you aim; most parents and coaches have said to aim for the back rim or middle rim, some even say aim for the backboard or square. I believe in the front rim as the front rim ensures a soft shot. Back rim ensures kids will shoot it hard, or a brick, or hit the backboard hard... The back board should not be used for shooting unless you're in close or at the back board angle which is near the box in the lane or off the lane at a 45 degree angle. When you aim for the front rim sometimes you shoot air balls; air balls are good at shooting instead of bricks. Some of the best shooters I've seen or played against are listed below

1-   - **Dell Curry**- it seemed like he flipped it, it never stayed in his hand for a long time. He also had a quick release which ensured he could get his shot off against anyone. He was slow and non athletic but at 6-8 he could shoot his shot any time. My senior year at Iowa I saw him win a playoff game against the Celtics on a last second 3 point shot where it seemed like the ball was barely in his hand before he shot it.

2-   **Dale Ellis**- a pure jump shooter, form and all; he had great follow through, he shot a real jump shot so he had deep range as he was about 6- 8 as well. He had a strong upper body so it seemed like he almost shot like he pumped it. I see him each year at our NBA retired players annual meeting and he has shooting camps of his own. I want to bring Kenya to his camp very badly so she can learn from one of the all time best shooters in the NBA.

3 - **Tracy Murray** , I first met Tracy at an AAU tourney when we were 17years old in Los Angeles in early August. He was a tall gangly 6- 7 kid who wore size 17 shoes and was weak physically and un athletic but man could he stroke it and often gave shooting clinics at campuses when he was older and only miss 3 or 4 shots in an hour while talking. When he was at UCLA; and me at Iowa we both tried out for the World games under 21 team. As guys were messing around playing horse before our daily practices I saw him once shoot jump shot from half court, yes and actual jump shot. The one thing about Tracy's shot it always came off his hand perfectly, the seams, the rotation, off hand follow thru. I have a basketball card of him he signed when we played for the Toronto Raptors framed and he's shooting in the card and everything is perfect.

4- **Troy Skinner** at Iowa who played with me might have been the best pure shooter I played with at Iowa. We were freshman together and all anyone heard was how this small white kid from upstate small town Iowa could shoot the lights out. He set the all time Iowa high school record of 3's made per season, all time and in Iowa High School State Tournament games. His problem was that he just had a super slow release and it was a set shot, not to mention he shot a push shot off his chin. His dad was the great Coach **Alton Skinner** and won many games and state championships. How he let his own son shoot that bad fundamental shot is beyond me. Kind of brings me back to my own daughter and me knowing that if she was to play later on in life I had to change her shot. So back to Troy at Iowa; at times we had in the late Des Flood, a prominent shooting coach in the California Area who **Dr. Tom** used in his Stanford days. **Des** would come a few times a year when he had game breaks over holidays and work with us with our free throws and the guards and wings would shoot 3 pointers. With Troy, I remember **Des** and Coach **Gary Close** saying Troy get the ball up. With Troy's size he had to get the ball up to get his shot off but rarely ever did. He was never able to duplicate any of the 3 point success he had in high school because of his low shot form and he couldn't get his shot off against bigger, taller, faster, Big Ten competition.

5- - **Brad Lohaus** and **Matt Bullard**-both played at Iowa and at 7-0 and at 6-10 shot over the defense and had an unblockable shot. Both had pure shooting forms, and made many 3's at Iowa and in the NBA. Brad was a league leader in 3 point shots with the Celtics and Bucks and was able to stretch the big lumbering centers of the early nineties away from the basket. Matt also had a great NBA career as he played with the Houston Rockets many years during the Hakeem Olajuwon and Clyde Drexler days. As teams doubled them he was able to stand at the top of the 3 point line and drill about 2-3 a game. At Iowa, I was a red shirt freshman when he played and to see him shoot in practice and warm ups was a pretty sight for a big man to shoot like that. Both inspired me to go to Iowa and work on my shot and one of my favorite shots to shoot is the top of the circle 3 point shot on the semi break trailing the play like Matt and Brad used to shoot. In fact back in 1999 I was home in the winter as I was bouncing around from overseas team to team and I played in an Iowa City Recreation league and Brad played on a team as well. He was semi retired and I was still in top game shape and he lit me up for about 5-6 threes. It was so bad 1 guy on my team called time out and said we need to guard the tall blond headed guy!

6 - **Seth Curry**-the son of **Dale Curry**. Probably the next great shooter in the young up-and-coming players. His story is unique as his dad held him back from AAU/travel team ball every weekend and only held him to 1 tourney a month. He then worked on his shot to improve his shot each day as the other local kids were screwing around in meaningless tourneys and practices. His shot is impeccable and often uses a quick release and high arc like his dad.

7- - **Kobe Bryant**- often not looked upon as a shooter because of his scoring ability and athletic ability, but might have the purest jump shot in the NBA now. He has worked hard to perfect his shot and often rents out gyms with shooting coaches and rebounders to perfect his shot. As mentioned above, his tireless work ethic to be better than **Jordan**, has propelled him to work on his shot. I love watching him shoot and he always follows through, even on bad misses, his form still is steady.

8- - **Kevin Durant** - despite being 6-9 he plays shooting guard and small forward, shoots like a guard. He always wanted to play guard and forward when he was a kid and rumor has it, when his AAU coach told him to go to the post in the 8th grade he said no I want to play wing despite being the tallest kid on the team. His coach therefore told him if he wanted to play wing he had to work on his shot. As Durant lived near the boys and girls club where they practiced he'd live in the gym from that day forward. Watching him shoot sometimes is like art as the ball seems to not hit the rim and net sometimes. His key is a quick pull up, meaning that he gets the ball from dribble position to shot form and release faster than almost anyone in the game. Many can do it, but often the ball might get hitched in your hand or set the wrong way, almost like a gunslinger in a shootout. You may pull the gun out of your holster fast but is it straight and ready to fire? Durant is ready to fire every time.

9- **Glenn Robinson** aka Big Dog. One of my all time favorites as he at 6-9 could shoot the seams off the ball. Glenn only wanted to shoot, that was his problem, he didn't want to work on his total game, but when he shot it was pretty. He had a hitch where it kind of pumped and caught the defender off guard. He shot kind of over his head a little bit and shot it often. So his speed and trajectory was different, as it was almost a fast jump shot. He was from Gary, Indiana and often played in many charity and streetball games when most NBA players didn't play in such games. I once heard a story from a guy I played with on the Boston Celtics, **Tony Harris** who also was from Gary who hosted his charity game and he said Glenn had 40+ points in a game, on all 3 pointers and jump shots with no layups or dunks.

10- **Dirk Nowitzki**. At 7-0 Dirk is the epitome that the overseas player explosion in the 90s and then learning and mastering the fundamentals of the game was way more important than dunking and highlight plays. When Dirk came into the league he was a league leader after a few years in 3 pointers made and taken. He shoots on the way down and over his head and he shoots cross seemed. The only great shooter I ever saw shoot cross seamed since **Reggie Miller**. Dirks 25+ free throws in a row during a NBA finals game versus the Miami Heat a few years ago is a record I'm not so sure we will ever see again.

<u>Coach Walker's Offensive Footwork</u>

I. General Consideration of Offensive Footwork

    a. In executing any individual move properly the player must be in a crouch position. Knees bent, backside down, back straight, and head up. This gives the player good body balance and control and permits quick, effective execution of the drive, the pass, or the outside shot.

    b. Efficient movement depends upon body control and timing NOT speed.

    c. A player may be an outstanding shooter but if he cannot maneuver to get open once the defensive man is on him, he is just another average player who cannot take advantage of his shooting skills.

    d. Everyone must be made to understand the significance, importance, and execution of proper footwork not only with the ball but without the ball to free himself for a pass, in cutting to the basket, in getting open for the shot, to set up screens, and to use screens.

    e. Moving without the ball part of the offense is vital for without this ability there would be no ball handling opportunities. Basketball is a game of motion. Don't be a ball beg.

    f. Keep your man busy, do not just stand there and expect to be part of the offense. Remember the easiest man to defend is the one who moves in a straight line; the most difficult one to defend is the one who can stop, start, change directions, and execute turns.

    g. Intelligent basketball players vary their fakes and feints with no fake movement. A player using this tactic merely bursts past the defensive man without a fake. In this way a good player does not type himself. The defensive player must be on his toes and must play the offensive man honest as he is uncertain what the offensive player is going to do: fake? No fake? Which is the best fake to use ? Do not let the defensive man "get a read" on you.

    h. Types of Stops

        i. Stride stop

            1. Excellent for quick stops; natural way to stop

            2. Come to a dead stop, breaking the forward motion with

the forward foot, body weight back, center of
gravity low.
3. Hold the ball with both hands with proper finger
control, elbows close to the body.
4. Stop with the knee of the forward foot well bent;
rear leg almost straight.
5. Remain in a semi-crouch position as long as ball
possession is retained. Protect the ball with your
body. Good body balance. Rear foot pivot foot.
6. If using the dribble, end the dribble simultaneously
with the stop.

ii. Square Stop

1. Best type of stop for normal speed forward motion.
Advantage lay in the fact that you can establish
either foot as the pivot foot.
2. Jab step and rocker steps (including hesitation
step) utilized best from this type of stop.
3. Come to stop, breaking your forward motion with feet
in a parallel or squared position. Weight evenly
distributed. Semi-crouch position. Good body balance.
Elbows close to the body.
4. Protect the ball by keeping it close in on your body.
Finger control.

II. Pivoting

a. There are so many occasions in basketball when a pivot is
helpful that pivoting should be taught as a separate skill, just as
we teach other fundamentals.
b. Pivoting is a weapon that can be used by every member of the
team whether he has the ball or not.
c. Pivoting practice also causes a player to gain better body balance;
they learn to stay low with legs bent; pivoting practice helps in
the development of stops and starts; and it will cut down on the
number of footwork errors.
d. The pivot is used to protect and retain possession of the ball; to

outmaneuver and work around stubborn defensive men, and to work away from the sidelines and out of corners.

e. Once the pivot foot has been established, you cannot pick up this foot from the floor or else you will lose possession of the ball. This pivot foot, however, can be pivoted but this move must be made on the ball of the foot without moving or sliding this foot across the floor. A pivot move is a spinning movement off the ball of your
foot.

f. If you come to a square or parallel stop, either foot may be established as the pivot foot; if you come to a stride stop (one foot in advance of the other), the rear foot will be the pivot foot. However, in the stride stop if the dribbler does not pick up (stop) his dribble until the front foot strikes the floor then either foot may be established as the pivot foot. Naturally the man without the ball can establish either foot to be used as the pivot foot regardless of the stance in which he stops.

g. **The Front Pivot**
   i. Dribbler advances to the defensive man and comes to a stride stop with one foot in advance of the other.
   ii. As the stop is made the rear of the body is brought low to maintain balance. Knees are bent.
   iii. The rear foot is established as the pivot foot.
   iv. The forward foot is swung in an arc to the front and across the pivot foot as the pivot is being made on the ball of the rear foot.
   v. During this move weight is on the rear or pivot foot.
   vi. When the front or forward foot strikes the floor the weight is shifted from the pivot foot to this foot.
   vii. The turn can be made by executing turns of 90 degrees: one- quarter (90 degrees); one-half (180 degrees); three-quarters (270 degrees); and full (360 degrees).
   viii. Most commonly used pivot is the one-quarter pivot.

h. **The Reverse Pivot**
   i. Sometimes referred to as the trailer pivot.
   ii. Dribbler advances to the defensive man and comes to a stop

in a stride position.

iii. As the stop is being made the rear of the body is brought low to maintain balance. Knees are bent.

iv. The rear foot is established as the pivot foot.

v. The forward foot is swung in an arc to the rear and in back of the pivot foot as the pivot is being made on the ball of the rear foot. Weight is on the pivot foot.

vi. As the front foot strikes the floor weight is shifted to the front foot.

vii. This pivot can be made by executing turns of one-quarter, one-half, three-quarters, and full.

III. Offensive Fakes and Footwork

A. Jab Step

i. Best to begin from a solid square stance but also can be executed proficiently from a straddle stance also.

ii. Move one foot rapidly forward or to the side one-half or one-quarter of a step. If in the straddle stance this forward movement must be made on the forward foot.

iii. Quickly return the foot to its original position. Make movements on the ball of the foot with the heel is slightly raised from the floor.

iv. Both knees are bent about 50%.

v. Protect the ball by carrying it on the hip or leg you are jab stepping with.

vi. Once the defensive man has reacted to this step, jab off his front foot to beat him. In other words if his right foot is forward, drive left; if his left foot is forward, drive right. If the defensive man reacts in a normal defensive position, your drive to the basket will then need a crossover step.

vii. If the defensive man does not react to cover the side you are jab stepping to, thendrive immediately off that 1st step.

B. The Rocker Step

viii. Best to begin from a square stance but again can be executed proficiently from straddle step stance also. If in the stride stance, the first step forward must be made on the forward foot.

ix.   Used by the ball handler before he has dribbled to fake the defensive man off balance for either a drive or a shot. This is a very effective offensive weapon to get the defensive player off balance.

x. Hold the ball with both hands protecting it on the hip on the side of the rocker step part of the body in a semi-crouch position.

xi. Use head and shoulder fakes while taking steps forward for a fake drive.

xii.   As the defensive man retreats into defensive position, the offensive man draws his forward foot back and brings the ball into a shooting position. Make certain the knees are bent about 50%. If the defensive man fails to recover after the fake, then you take the shot.

xiii.   If the defensive man makes a rush to prevent the shot, the offensive man drives forward with the same foot toward the basket. Try to work off the defensive man's forward foot using either the cross-over or jab step. It is depending upon the position of the defensive man's forward foot.

C. The Hesitation Step

xiv.   A variation of the rocker step but much slower.

xv.   In this movement the offensive player takes the step forward and then backwards (in a rocker movement).

xvi.   After taking the rocker step movement, the offensive player takes a quick hesitation step of about a half-a-step in length forward. Then the offensive bursts by the defensive man with a driving dribble.

xvii. The hesitation followed by the burst of speed forward can act as a surprise move to the basket.

b. Change of Directions Move

i. It is Used to rid yourself of an aggressive defensive player. It can be used with or without the ball. To use with the dribble, see notes above on dribbling.

ii. The Offensive man cuts hard in one direction and stops with one foot in front of the other. The forward foot is the decoy foot to go away from the direction you wish to go.

iii. Push off the ball of this foot hard while the rear step (low and short) moves in the direction you wish to go. The Forward foot follows in a long cross over stride.

E. Change of Pace Move

iv.   Can be used with or without the dribble.

v. Simple movements in varying the speed so that the defensive man will go by the offensive man.

vi. Start fast, slow down, and then speed up or Reverse the procedure.

vii.   Develop both short and full strides with good body balance and control.

F-The Reverse Move

viii.   Used to shake an aggressive or overplaying defensive man. The Move is used without the ball and most often by forwards along the baseline. Also an effective move for the man under the basket and the man in the foul circle/lane.

ix.   Usually referred to as "pulling the string" or "backdoor move". All teams should have a pre-set signal to let the passer know that the offensive man intends to use this move (tug of the shirt,or eye signal etc).

x. The offense forward cuts to meet the pass. It is Very important that the passer fakes the pass to further draw the defensive man closer to the defender.

xi. The tightly guarded player jump stops with the leg next to the defender forward to hold him off from getting the ball. If you do receive the pass then the priority is to protect the ball.

xii.   Push off the lead foot as you "feel" the side of the defensive man.

xiii.   Pivot to the outside on your rear foot turning in the opposite direction of your forward foot. The Forward foot coming in front of and around your pivot foot.

xiv.   Take a full step to the rear, while shifting the body weight evenly on both feet as you make the quick cut to the basket.

F. The Cross-Over Step

xv.   Often Used to shake a close-guarding defensive man or by the ball handler before he has dribbled to fake his defensive man out.

There are many fakes associated with the cross-over step.

xvi. FAKE RIGHT, GO LEFT

1. With moving the pivot foot to the left, the offensive man fakes a drive to the right by jab stepping to the right with his right foot.

2. He quickly pivots on his left foot and at the same time crosses his right foot in a long, low stride across the defensive player's lead foot. The first step on the drive left will be with his right foot. Right shoulder (shoulder nearest to the defensive man) is lowered and the body protects the ball.

3. Remember that you cannot pick up your pivot foot; therefore the first step must be with your right foot.

4. In all crossover moves explained here and below, keep in mind that whenever you intend to dribble the ball on these crossover moves the dribble. It must be accompanied by the cross-over step to protect the ball from the defender. The dribble must hit the floor before you pick up your pivot foot or its a travel.

xvii. FAKE LEFT, GO RIGHT

Same steps as above only reverse the feet and direction of the fakes and dribbles.

xviii. FAKE RIGHT, GO RIGHT

1. The Dribbler or ball handler fakes a drive to the right by a cross-over step with his left foot and a fake of the ball.

2. He then stops and moves his head and shoulder back faking the drive to the left.

3. Then go Almost immediately to begin the dribble move. Push off with the right foot first and then go hard with the left hand drive as you drive to the hoop.

4. Use the Shoulder nearest to the defensive man. Lower the ball and make sure it is protected by the body.

xix. FAKE LEFT, GO LEFT

Same steps as above only reverse the feet and direction.

xx. FAKE RIGHT, FAKE LEFT, GO RIGHT

1. Ball handler first fakes right by bringing the ball and
    the

left arm across the front of the defensive man.

    2. Then he pushes hard with the left foot to push his body back to the left.   Then pivot on his rear foot so it has to be a strong and a short quick step.

    3. The ball handler then pushes off the left foot with a cross-over step once again in front of the defensive man. (same as step 1) and drives to the basket.

xxi. FAKE LEFT, FAKE RIGHT, GO LEFT

    Same steps as above only reverse the feet and direction.

IV. Screening

a. General Considerations About Screening

    i. Screening is the backbone of modern basketball many coaches believe. All offenses use the screen in some manner when setting up their offenses.

    ii.. A screen is a temporary barrier, with body contact. The offensive man screens the defensive man for an offensive teammate.

    iii. The purpose of a screen is to impede the progress of the defensive man temporarily to:

        1. cause him to break stride

        2. lose him

        3. force him into a poorly timed switch with another defender.

        4. Or to get an easy shot.

    iv. Good fakes along with change of pace or change of directions can help to set up an effective screen.

    v. When setting an inside screen or a side screen go up close to the defender. Do not make hard contact when setting a screen.   The rules say you must give the defender sufficient room for him to take one normal step. See rules below.

    vi. The rules for screening state:

        1. If the screen is set within the visual field of a stationary opponent, the screener may be as close as possible, and short of contact.

        2. If the screen is set outside the visual field of a stationary opponent, the screener must permit the

opponent to take

at least one step. In order to set a good screen a player has to go toward the screen without making hard contact. This is one **normal** step to not move on the screen.

    3. If the opponent is moving, the screen must be set far enough in advance of the opponent to permit him to avoid contact and get at least 2 steps to avoid it. In no situation is it necessary to set the screen farther than two strides from the opponent.

vii. Timing is essential in all screens.

b. Types of Screens

  i. **Inside screen** occurs when a screener stops in a legal position **between** his teammate and his teammate's opponent. Particularly useful to set up a shot or a fake shot and drive for a better shot.

  ii. **Outside screen or back screen** occurs when a screener stops in a legal position directly **behind** a teammate's opponent. Used by forward or low man in screening for guards. Excellent weapon for the pick and roll move.

  iii. **Side screen** occurs when a screener stops in a legal position **beside** a teammate's opponent. Used particularly by guards on bigger opponents.

  iv. **Moving screen** occurs when an offensive man with or without the ball rubs off another moving offensive player. Often called a violation if not done properly. Difficult to execute but very effective. It Takes a great deal of timing to be effective.

c. Setting the Screen

  i. When setting a screen it is important to keep your feet set.

    1. Locate the man to be screened and wont move on the screen.

    2. Get close to him and spread out in a wide basketball stance.

    3. Either face him or turn your back to him but use your whole body.

    4. Stay set until the screen has been taken and then roll to the basket or pop out.

  ii. The Proper screening angle is necessary to prevent the

defensive man from sliding through your screen.

iii. The screener should stand hard and erect with a slight bend. Bend the knees to give good positioning to his body so that his head is in front. Line up to the defensive man's body rather than come from behind. Your Feet must be parallel and nice.

Please spread strong and approximately go slightly further apart than shoulder width for most effectiveness.

    iv. Do Stand immobile without leaning into the path or extending the hips into the path. Don't sway into the path of the defensive man. Arms and hands should hang naturally but strongly out from the sides of the body for protection. Be careful that they are not moved into the path of the defensive man.

    v. Be prepared for the contact as it could be rough. Once the defensive man makes contact **with you,** roll to the basket by executing a reverse pivot. By Opening your body up to the ball and the passer. Use the hand opposite the pivot foot high in anticipation of the pass

d. Using the Screen is important to be effective.

    i. The Man for which the screen is set must wait until the screen is set so that the screener will be stationary.

    ii. The Man for which the screen is set should develop a variety of fakes and footwork to use when coming off the screen or prior to coming off the screen.

    iii. Once the screen has been set it is the responsibility of the offensive man of which the screen has been set to cause his defensive man to run into the body of the screener.   In order to make it impossible for the defensive man to move through the screen with you setting it. The object is to Force the switch to big to small defenders.

    iv. When you rub off a screen try to brush the screener's arm or leg. This way there will be no room for the defensive man to get through the screen and catch up.

<u>**Coach Earl's Rebounding**</u>

Way back From the days of old school basketball, coaches at camps and clinics always taught position, technique, and some footwork for rebounding. Some of those things are true to be able to rebound the ball, but in my days of playing I've learned a few things differently. I played with and against some of the greatest rebounders to ever play the game which I will detail below. No particular order, just the best I ever saw or heard about or played against.

1. **Eddie Horton**, whom I played with when I was a freshman at University of Iowa, He was a senior, only 6-8 but only 240 pounds. But he was all muscle and was all Big Ten. You must have heart, desire, ability and a level of nastiness to be able to rebound at a high level. He was from Springfield, IL and his dad was serving a life sentence for drugs and other offenses and ended up dying in prison. Eddie was a mean dude on the court and would not back down from anyone. He would push, grab and elbow you constantly under the basket for the ball. He was limited offensively, so offensive rebounding was his way to score. He could jump a little bit as I had only seen him dunk two-handed one time. His rebounding edge was to use his butt AND body and he had great timing. I once saw him punk out and out play **J.R. Reid** from the University of North Carolina.   In the Dean Dome was the game, as he recorded 22 rebounds on National TV his Senior year when we beat North Carolina.

2. **Bill Russell** was a great rebounder and maybe the best of all time. He was only 6-8 as well but he was somewhat very athletic and could jump very high with a 40 inch vertical leap. Russell used his head to position himself against taller and stronger guys. He boxed out more than any other rebounders, which meant that he put his body between the other man and the basket. Players had to often go over his back or push him out the way to get a rebound, which was a foul on the other guy. His duels with Wilt Chamberlain were legendary. He had many games with 20 and 30+ rebounds in the playoffs and championship games. His will to sacrifice scoring and to play defense is legendary.

3. **Wilt Chamberlain**, with being 7-1 and strong and tall, and the greatest athlete over 6-9 ever to play in the NBA. Wilt used his leaping ability and athleticism to get the ball, score and dominate the game. He often beat players to the ball using his quickness and

jumping ability. He was an all American track star at the University of Kansas in the long jump, high jump, hurdles and relays. Some coaches and analysts even speculated that he could still play in the 90s and today if he was alive and in playing shape. For him to get 20, 30 and 40 rebound games were a drop in the bucket for him. Even against Bill Russell who was the best defensive player of all time he often dominated him.

4. **Charles Barkley** was probably the best rebounder for his size at any level. Barkley was only 6-4 but was listed at 6-6. Early in his career Barkley had great quickness and jumping ability despite playing overweight most of his career. In his peak though, he would use his body to get great rebounding numbers. He was nasty and often out- rebounded bigger and stronger players at the power forward or center position. He was never afraid to mix it up under the basket and often got flagrant fouls and technical for throwing his weight around. Some funny YouTube clips were him mixing it up with **Xavier McDaniel, Kevin Mchale, Bill Laimbeer** and **Shaq among others**. He is one of the stars who thought that by rebounding big numbers would and could change the outcome of the game.

   Even today he often calls out superstars in big games when they don't rebound well in big games. His career with the Phoenix Suns he had some very big rebounding playoff games. Especially one game versus the Houston Rockets or Seattle Supersonics where he had 30 rebounds in a game 7 of the Western Conference Playoffs. One game when I played with the Toronto Raptors I was lined up for a free throw rebound with him. He was the inside player closest to the rim. He got the rebound and I thought I could go over his back and maybe tip it back to me. As soon as I grazed the ball he snatched it in and turned a bit to me and gave me a elbow swipe across my face about 1 or 2 inches away. He was just letting me know he could've taken me out if he wanted, by sending a message. Lol, there is a picture someplace of that as I saw it in a Toronto paper a few days later with me giving the [ooh wee] face as he swung his elbow to my face.

5. **Dennis Rodman** was maybe the best rebounder of all time or in the modern era. He was a skinny guy out of a D-2 school and was 6-9ish but very thin. He had a motor, meaning he often moved his feet so that he never stood still. He was an average jumper and Rarely dunked.   But as his career surfaced he found out rebounding was his forte. He was a high energy guy for the Bad

Boys - NBA Detroit Pistons when they won the back to back championships with **Isaiah Thomas** and **Joe Dumars**, and **Bill Laimbeer**, etc. Of all the rebounders I listed above, he was the worst offensive skill player listed. Even sometimes by not scoring or even attempting a basket or shots at times. Playing against him, he'd use his quick feet to get inside you. Or he would hit you first to bump you off balance, then quickly get the ball off a rebound. When he played With the Spurs he put up great rebounding numbers.   When he was with the Chicago Bulls he understood he was the last option on offense and behind **Michael Jordan**, **Scottie Pippen**, and **Toni Kukoc**, etc. I even think he had a few games in a row where he never attempted a shot. He was a player in my opinion who created the dribble out to the top and gave the ball back to the point guard on an offensive rebound. When I was growing up I was taught to put it back up and draw a foul or get a 3 point play under the basket.   But the defense

was not set, but since he didn't want to score he'd dribble it back out and give it back to **M.J. Kerr** or **Pippen**. If you look at games on T.V. Now at each level, the best rebounder often dribbles it back out rather than shoot it back up. I even saw a WNBA player do that in the playoffs from the Minnesota Lynx as she gave it back to **Mya Moore** for a quick 3 point shot. Rodman created that action we all see today.   **Rodman** would also hit you 1st on a rebound, even on an offensive rebound. The ball would be in an offensive player's hand and they might be ready to shoot.   But he would start moving when the player has not yet shot yet. **Rodman** would hit you then release or even grab and hold you but act like he wasn't. He has tons of footage where he's holding the other guy during a shot or rebound and got into tons of skirmishes with guys.

6. **Moses Malone** was probably my favorite rebounder of all time. He often grabbed double digit rebounds and scored well to put up 20- 20 games (meaning 20 points and 20 rebounds). No players have been able to do that since **Wilt Chamberlain** and **Bill Russell.** He was often not duplicated now until **Kevin Love** in the modern day game of basketball could do that. Moses often missed his own shots on purpose to pad his stats or just get closer to the rim and then score. He was a better offensive rebounder than a defensive rebounder but a good player as well. Moses prided himself in being in good shape. I remember when my old Iowa teammate **Roy Marble** played for the Atlanta Hawks with Moses he often tried to get Roy to work out and get in better shape. Even when you hear **Barkley** on TNT, he credits **Malone** in getting him in shape to play top level NBA basketball. Moses thought if he was in great game shape he would outlast the opposing centers

as the game goes by and over an 82 game season and the playoffs. Even today as I saw
him each year at the NBA retirement annual meetings he looked

like he

still plays. There was Not an ounce of fat on him, as he looked like he was still at his playing weight of around 235 lbs. he would often joke with me on eating alot and drinking late. I remember when I was a rookie with the Boston Celtics, **Robert Parrish** told me that he was the hardest player to guard because you had to constantly box him out all game. Later on when I played for the Toronto Raptors we were playing against the San Antonio Spurs and late in the 3rd quarter I came in to play due to some foul trouble to our Celtic big men.   **Moses** was at the end of his career around his 19- or 20th year. I thought in his old age I didn't have to box him out or even worry about him for a rebound. Little did I know he was still as quick and slick as ever. On every rebound, whenever there was a chance for both of us to get it, he got it. I was so bad boxing him out our coach called a time out to tell me alone to box him out.   I remember their bench players were laughing at me because I couldn't box him out. In 2 or 3 minutes of the 3rd quarter he had about 5 or 6 rebounds and all on me. Last time I seen him was New Orleans NBA retired players meetings. We hung out and ate a late dinner one time, he asked the waiter about 15 minutes on how each entre was cooked. He was in great shape and told me dont be afraid to ask those questions. He later died that year, by heart attack around the age of 55. Very sad, hurt my heart.

7. **Popeye Jones**—I played with him on the Toronto Raptors and played against him when he was with the Dallas Mavericks. **Popeye** was only 6-7 but had a round pudgy body and used his quickness and head to put his body in front of yours. He'd put up big numbers in his career despite playing on bad and subpar teams. Pop was a great guy also and never got into scuffles which is kind of odd for such a great rebounder. He just wanted to rebound. He wasn't trying to ever grab you or elbow you or push you and play dirty. He was maybe the nicest rebounder you'd ever see or play against. He just wanted to rebound and did it very well.

   I first met Pop at the Olympic trials for the Jr. World games back when we were in college in the 90-91 season. Even he was a great rebounder back then at Murray State. We often stayed up at night and hosted mini parties with Grant Hill, Ervin Johnson, Travis Ford etc when we traded gear and told stories. When we played together In Toronto Raptors we lived in the same building and drove to the airport together for some home games. A great player and friend and now an assistant coach in the NBA.

8. **Kevin Love**- he's the modern day **Moses Malone** but a better shooter and not a scoring threat like **Malone** was under the hoop but more of a perimeter threat. Some have compared him to **Larry Bird** on his shooting and knack for the ball. **Kevin** has a great motor as well as he has to come from far away from the basket to rebound the ball. He's a great 3 point shooter and passer so he's always hanging out by the 3 point line on offense but still rebounds the ball very well. His running starts some say has helped him to get angles that most rebounders don't have. He's lost some weight to be quicker as well but not a great jumper. He uses his position very well and also I think some players

underestimate him around the basket. They thought he was a slow white guy and could not out jump African Americans. He put up a back to back 30 rebound games 1 season which hasn't been done since the 80s or 90s.

9. **Reggie Evans** – last but not least from Iowa. He's put up great rebounding numbers at Iowa despite only playing a few years at Iowa. He went into the NBA undrafted and worked his way into playing for at least 7-9 NBA teams and seasons. He often digs out rebounds for the stars he's played with so they can shoot again. Stars such as **Chris Paul, Allen Iverson, Rashard Lewis, Ray Allen, Carmelo Anthony**, and **Deron Williams often loved him**. He got them extra shots and then he would dribble the ball right to them on an offensive rebound. **Reggie** was a little nasty and not afraid to do what it takes to grab the ball, or balls lol. just YouTube or Google the story about when he grabbed **Chris Kaman** in the male genital area on a rebound in the playoffs when he played for the Seattle SuperSonics.

We always had battles in the old field house playing pickup ball when he was still at the University of Iowa and I was back and forth from playing overseas during the summers. Then we battled in the summers at the Prime Time league. He'd try to beat the crap out of me and hold and grab me for rebounds. One game he had 10 fouls as you couldn't foul out. A reporter was doing a story on us both so he kept the stats of
the game and was amazed on how he could have all his fouls on me lol. He then reported all the fouls he committed were against me and Reggie was very mad about it, I told him dudes in the Big Ten who were all big ten couldn't guard me so why was he surprised lol. We never got along too much socially but as a player I respect him and was very proud he had a long career in the NBA. He was the only Iowa Hawkeye still playing in the NBA for many years. When he played on TV I often found myself just watching him to see all the times he grabbed and held guys like he did me. He still can't score around the basket nor make a free throw but he's found his niche. Coaches and players loved him as a teammate indeed.

To sum it all up, if you have the chance to grab the ball, go get it; any way you can. All the guys listed above were not fundamental box out guys. Just because you're a taller, bigger, or faster player does not mean you're going to be a great rebounder. Shaq O'Neill, Kareem Abdul-Jabbar, and even

I were not great rebounders for the height or skill sets we all had despite being very tall. With them being such great centers, they had some of the worst rebounding numbers for a center over their career. Also, just because you're a good jumper doesn't mean you'll be able to rebound as well. Such as Vince Carter,or his cousin Tracy Mcgrady, wing players that were barely able to rebound their position. Just because you're strong doesn't mean you'll be good at rebounding either. When I played overseas for 8 years, a lot of times I didn't have plays called for me so I had to go get the ball to be able to score. I became a good-great rebounder later in my career.

<u>Coach Walker's The Fast Break</u>

I. General Considerations of the Fast Break

    a. The fast break is a controlled or racehorse style of play. It should be carefully planned and a skillfully executed maneuver to get good shots.

    b. Types of fast break we will list below.

        i. **A Controlled fast break** occurs when a team breaks **only** on such occasions.   Such as an excellent opportunity to beat the defense down court (to outnumber them) when it presents itself.

        ii. **Streetball break** occurs when a team forces the fast break situation on every occasion even when they do not have favorable numbers. Their purpose is to get the ball up court as quickly as possible every time they gain possession of the ball. In streetball they often go 2 vs 3 or 3 vs 4 when it does not make sense to engage in defense.

    c. Objectives

        i. To take advantage of turnovers caused by defensive pressure.

        ii. To attempt to break the game open when the offense has a lead.

        iii. To demoralize the opposition and take their will.

        iv. To overcome a height advantage and play small and use quickness and or shooting.

        v. To change the tempo of the game if your team is playing slow and stagnant.

    d. The Main Ingredients Necessary for Fast Break Play.

        i. Teamwork as everyone has to do their job.

        ii. Timing and coordination, everyone has to be in the right spot at the right time.

        iii. Alertness and determination to conquer the team goals

        iv. Pride and a high degree of concentration for each game.

        v. Excellent physical conditioning, as fast break teams have to be in the best shape from each player.

        vi. . A positive attitude to keep up the fast break at all costs is needed by the whole team.

    e. Defending the Fast Break is mostly hard for many teams.

i. Aggressive offensive rebounding can stop the fast break.
ii. Aggressive coverage of the most prominent defensive rebounder with a double team can be effective.
iii. Prevention or delaying the outlet pass can stop the fast break.
iv. Stopping the man with the ball as fast as possible when or before they get the ball is key.
v. Maintain good floor balance on defense and do not alow open paths to the basket. Have a full ccheck man (usually a forward depending upon the situation) in a position at the top of the key and a half check man (either a

guard or a forward depending upon the situation) at the side of the lane foul line near the elbow area. This man can pick up long rebounds and loose balls coming his way. They are able to beat the defensive man down the floor, helping to prevent the fast break.

vi.   If you get caught in a two-on-one situation, stay in the middle of the lane. Using the defensive mentality to make the dribbler pick up his dribble or commit himself as far as away as possible. Drop back to shut off the passing lane to the other offensive man.

vii.   If you get caught in a three-on-one situation, use the same maneuvers as in the two-on-one situation and try to take a charge or steal the pass or even strip the ball from the player but don't gamble.

viii.   If you get caught in a three-on-two situation, line up in tandem (one behind the other) with the lead man slightly above the free throw line. The second man should be halfway to the basket area. The Lead man's duty is to stop the ball as high up as possible and make the offense pass or pick up the dribble early. The second or low man picks up the lead pass while the original high man drops low to guard the basket. Again tandem) to shut off feed for a layup to the third offensive man.

II. Fast Break Starting Points

    a. Defensive Rebounding

        i. Be aware of rebounding and lane responsibilities and cut off easy paths quickly.

        ii. Watch for the long rebound as it can trigger the fast break.

        iii. Execute a good outlet pass to start the break.

    b. Pressing Defensive Maneuvers.

        i. Players should Be very aware of rebounding and lane responsibilities and execute quickly to stop offensive advantages.

        ii. The offensive Man closest to the ball should take the ball out of bounds once the official has handed the ball to them or on a made basket. They should take a quick look under the basket or down court 1st for pressing defense. The others running to the offense end looking for quick passes to score and or push the ball ahead.

iii. Especially this is significant on violations in the back court of the opposition.

iv. Be prepared for the break after a deflected pass, a steal, blocked shot or an interception. Upon gaining possession of the ball, look up court to the others sprinting to offense and looking for a quick pass.

c. After a Scored goal or foul shot.

    i. The Man nearest the ball should take the ball out of bounds and look deep ball side for the 1st initial pass.   The others sprint to the offense side looking for a quick pass upcourt.

    ii. It is best to have Usually a prearranged offensive maneuver for a fast break like positions and or duties for each player on the court.

d. The Controlled Tip or tap out.

    i. The main rebounders or big guys will Tap the ball forward to the guard around the old hash mark area or near the free throw line. Then the tapper fills the third and last lane on the fast break.

    ii. This is Usually a prearranged offensive maneuver often practiced and drilled in practice. When I played in highschool there was a team in our conference Quincy high school that used that.

III. Fundamentals to be Mastered for the Successful Break.

a. Passing is key to limit turnovers.

    i. The Ball should always be passed forward except when in the scoring area and zones.

    ii. . A good beginning leads to a successful ending especially in Vegas lol.

    iii. Make sure there is Sharp, crisp, and quick passing.

    iv. These are the Types that are very Important

        1. Outlet pass to beat players down the floor.

        2. Two-Handed Overhead to pass over the defense.

        3. Hook pass to pass around the defender.

        4. Chest pass for short close passes.

        5. Baseball passes to pass long up the floor.

        6. Bounce pass to pass lower than tall defenders

b. Dribbling can be key but not important.

    i. Use the Dribble only when a pass is impossible to use.

ii. Players Must be ready to use both hands on their dribble
moves, with the right and left hand equally.
iii. These are the Types that are Important.
1. Change of Speed.
2. Change of Direction
c. Shooting is more important than ever since the game is now outside
in.
i. Take the first good shot; do not waste time if you have a good

shot, take it even if it is a quick 3-point shot..

    ii. These Types are very Important to be a good fast break team.

        1. Layup, especially the underhand layup and now the floater or Euro-step.

        2. Jump Shot from the foul line/elbow area called the mid-range shot.

        3. Jump Shot from the side below the foul line sometimes called the wing area.

        4. TAP-IN, or tip in in order to put the ball in the hoop off the rebound.

        5. Foul Shooting can stop the fast break and can set up the defense with a zone and or press defense.

d. Offensive Footwork is key now to not travel.

    i. Each player needs to Run as fast as possible is key to be effective. Both with the forwards and guards to push the ball into the frontcourt.

    ii. The main ball handler should use Stops, starts, and change of acceleration to get other players easy shots.

    iii. Pivoting can be important if players jump and stop off the dribble. Villanova and the great coach Jay Wright taught his players to jump-stop and pivot to find shooters outside.

    iv. It is very important to teach offensive players to jab step and pump fake in the lane to draw fouls.

    v. Fakes and footwork is very important to play outside the lane and on the wing.

        1. Cross over steps are important for every offensive player.

        2. Change of Direction and change if speed is important to score.

        3. Change of Pace and speed is key to keep the defenders off guard.

e. By Receiving the Ball and especially on the move is important to make sure your footwork is solid.

f. Peripheral vision is key for the point/lead guard to see all the passing angles and defenders.

g. Jump Ball Techniques are a thing of the past now days as scoring off the jump ball and 1st is not as important but can be in an

important game.
h. Pressing Defensive Principles are important to stop the fast break.

IV. Executing the Fast Break again needs all the players on the floor to buy in.
a. Aggressive rebounding, defense, jumping and having athletic players are very important to create situations to initiate the fast break.
b. The 1st Outlet pass to the release man must be mastered and executed with precision and quickness to beat the defense.
c. To Fill in least of three offensive lanes as rapidly as possible is key for a good fast break.
    i. You must Assume the lane nearest you is yours to fill when the ball comes into your team's possession. All teammates must be willing to fill other lanes.
    ii. All players must Maintain proper floor balance at all times and not overload the floor.
    iii. The offensive team must try to Keep the ball in the middle of the floor. In situations involving three offensive men or more the key is space on the floor on each wing and the middle. The Middleman or lead ball handler should definitely have the ball to see all passing and scoring options. When they approach the top of the key they should see shooters and post player options to pass to.
    iv. Wingmen should spread out as wide as possible. They should not be coming together at any cost to not bring the defense to each other.

The defensive we don't want to come close enough to cover two areas or multiple players. Do not bring your man toward the man with the ball unless he is in difficulty or a scoring position.

v. The corners in modern day basketball have become the most important area in the game as it's the closest 3 pt line to the basket. Modern day teams should have at least 1 player in each corner as possible.

Approximately also have players near the foul line high up or slightly lowered to the mid and low post. Wing men should continue in their lanes cutting toward the basket until they reach the base line or in the lane. Then if they don't get the ball they should continue to the 3pt line to space the floor for other teammates.

d. Take the Good Shot or wait for the best shot.

i. Layups are the key for fast breaks.

ii. Foul line jumpers are the worst shot in fast break action.

iii. Side/elbow foul line jumpers are again not good shots in fast break basketball.

V. Common Fast Break Situations teams and players face.

a. Two-on-One/ ha a fun time indeed lol.

i. Spread it fairly wide to prevent the defensive man from playing both angles.

ii. Pass rapidly back and forth and go down the foul lines extended areas. When you come to the foul line extended, the man with the ball should dribble directly for the hoop and shoot if uncovered or pass if covered.

b. Three-on-One, ah ok lol.

i. Keep the ball in the middle, and spread it wide lol.

ii. Wingmen should cut to the basket when you get to the foul line extended. Players should Make Sharp cuts to the basket to score. See the section on filling the lanes above (IV and v).

iii. The Middle man should stop at the foul line and wait for a return pass from the middle man. Depending upon how the defensive man plays the options dictates what decisions the main ball handler makes. If the middle defender takes the ball below the foul line, they had better be able to shoot the ball and or create a shot for another player.

c. Three-on-Two-didn't we go through this before lol.

    i. See (I) and (ii) directly above are some ways to play it offensively and defensively.

    ii. Against a two-man zone type defense the offense should play for the fast break. The middle man should dribble down the middle to draw the defense for an open shot for your teammates or themselves.

    iii. Against the tandem defense, the middle man should stop at the foul line and await the return pass. But in the new game the player should pass and space out to the 3pt line for an open 3.

<u>**Coach Earl's Fast Break**</u>

The fast break in basketball is the fastest way to score. In the beginning of basketball after each score the teams would jump the ball again. So the idea was to score and pass before the defensive players got off the jump ball circle. Then after a score the opposing team would take the ball out quickly and try to pass the ball back down to the opposite basketball court. From day one, the fast break was always the fastest way to score.

John McClendon and **Piggy Lambert** were the pioneer coaches of the fast break. John along with Big House gains were the 1st two prominent black coaches and they both loved to press and fast break. Back in the 50-60's days, teams were the status quo with a lumbering center. To run the opposing team's center was the main idea to score before he got set back on defense. A lot of the old school coaches still believe the ball should not touch the floor when a team goes to fast break and scores. Some of the best fast break teams I ever seen and played against were below:

1- **UNLV** with **Coach Tarkanian**. His teams often led the nation in scoring and they won at least 30 games each year. Coach Tark actually came to visit Coach **Davis** at Iowa one summer to learn his thoughts on the fast break and how the press could work to fast break.

2- **University of Iowa** under Coach **Davis.** In his first season they went 30-5. They actually lost to UNLV in the Elite 8 Games after being up 17 points at half time. Coach Davis gave Coach Tark the blueprint to beat the press.

3- **Boston Celtics** of the 60's under the great point guard **Bob Cousy**. Those teams often scored from the fast break and seldom ran any plays.

4- **Los Angles** showtime Lakers of the 80's. Those teams I grew up on with **Magic Johnson, James Worthy, Michael Cooper,** and Kareem etc. Those teams were exciting to watch and ran teams literally out the gym each game.

5- **Paul Westphal's Loyola Marymount college team** - with **Hank Gathers** and **Bo Kimble**. Those teams led the NCAA in scoring and coach Westphal had a rule that the ball had to be shot in less than 5 seconds. The Lakers actually hired Westfahl before the great Pat Relily and that is how the Lakers got their fast break DNA.

6- **Grinnell College in Grinnell Iowa**- They set the record for most points in a NCAA game and a per game average. They used to keep two players on the other side of half court at each wing or corner at the 3 pt line. While the other three players were down playing a zone in a triangle formation. If the ball was stolen or a turnover occurred the ball was passed down quickly, even on a made basket for a quick three point shot. It did not matter on a made or missed basket, the ball was thrown down the court fast to get a quick three pointer. Every three minutes the coach would sub all five players out and all new players would come in. The coach would keep 25 plus players to keep his team fresh to play that style. Practice was totally optional. A few years ago they ditched that philosophy and just went to a 5 out and would not shoot layups, only 3's. One time a player scored like 80 plus pts in 1 game.

      7-**Mike D'Antoni's'** Phoenix Suns of the early 2000's-One of **D'Antoni's** rules was that the ball had to be shot in less than seven seconds. With the point guard the great **Steve**

Nash as the quarterback of their system, the Suns were exciting and fun to watch. They set records in scoring points per season, points in a quarter, in a half, etc. Most of the players at the time were all- stars and received huge contracts when they played for the Suns. Many went on to other teams and had subpar years because of not playing in a fast break system.

Even the great **Tom Davis** teams set records in the Big Ten and the NCAA before and when I played for Iowa. In one of my NCAA tournament games in the first round was against the University of Texas. At half time the score was tied at 70 points yes in 1992. We played two over-times and the final score was 120-125. Texas was a pressing fast break team also like us so the game was crazy. Both teams had 3 or 4 players with 25 plus pts.

Some good fast break drills to do are the (3-2) and (2-1). To start the drill there is a line of three players at the end line. Big guys are normally on the wings and guards are in the middle. The two players at the opposite end of the court are playing defense. The three offense players will come down to the two defensive players. The middle guy can dribble down or pass down the court as the offense runs down the floor. Then the other two players have to stop the other three players which is hard to do. The offense player who turns the ball over or misses the shot is now back on defense. The two defense players are now offensive players and pass and or dribble down to the opposite basket to score. The other two offensive players now become defense players. This is a great drill to speed up your players and to get your players to run, pass to the open player, change ends quickly, and to score quickly.

Another set of drills is to just do basic fast break full court drills. The point guard brings it up in the middle of the court, the the wings run wide to opposite sides of the court and out by the three point line. The first big player runs to the ball side block to post up maybe for an easy score. The second biggest player runs to the free throw line off to the elbow-ball side area. The whole process should take no longer than 2-4 seconds to get the ball up the floor and to pass to the other wing players. We are looking for easy wide open jump shots or dump downs to the ball side post. The key to the fast break is to make sure everyone knows where to run and space out. Most coaches think the fast break is just streetball or free lance, but it is not. When you have two posts run to the same side block or two wings run to the same side then obviously the spacing is bad and the defense can guard you more easily.

3-2 Fastbreak defense

2-1 Fastbreak

3-2 Fastbreak

<u>Coach Earl's Dribbling</u>

Dribbling is a key part of the game and now more than it ever once was. In the old days of hoops, the game was played with 1 conventional point guard. Then 1 shooting guard, 1 power forward, 1 small forward and 1 center. Back then, only the point guard handled the ball but now the game is different as we can see. Back then, the point guard was a small scrappy player and maybe just a smart kid with little talent.   Sometimes they are either the quarterback on the football team or a coach's son. Most times the most popular guy on the team or in the school everyone listened to and followed. Think back to **Nate Archibald, Chet Walker, Bob Cousy**, Steve Nash, John Stockton, Magic Johnson and **Calvin Murphy**. They all were premier point guards who changed the game.

Fast forward to 1979 when **Magic Johnson** came into the NBA. Magic was 6-9 and played point guard at Michigan State. He was Coached by the great **Jud Heathcothe who also recruited me in highschool.** He let him do whatever he wanted with the ball and it paid off. **Magic** thought like a guard and played like a guard, forward and center at 1 time. He changed the game to where now every big guy or forward thru the 90's thought or played like a guard. They all want to handle the ball and make plays.

The new NBA, AAU, College and high school, Every big time player handles the ball. The prominent players in the game now often bring the ball up the court or can go full court off the dribble with much skill. **Lebron** often plays point guard in key situations. **Kobe, Devin Booker, Anthony Davis, Big Kat,** and even **Kevin Garnett** were point forwards or guards in their prime.

Here are some of the best dribblers to ever play the game and change the game we know the day.

1. **Ralph Sampson** was maybe the first point forward at 7-4. He played at Virginia and is the only player in college history to ever win back to back college player of the year awards. Then he was drafted by the Houston Rockets and played for many years with them and the Kings. Coaches could not figure him out, as he always wanted to dribble and play away from the basket even though he was 7-4. I often said he came into basketball too early and his skill set was not suited for the old timer coaches in the 80's NBA. If he had a coach like **Don Nelson,** or even some of the progressive coaches of today such as **Avery Johnson, Doc Rivers, my ex wives fantasy lol, check her twitter profile. Imagine what Ralph could have done om todays game where 7 footers can now do what they want on the court.**

Ralph would've played longer and had more success if he played now in this era. He had Bill Fitch as a coach for a number of years and he was known as a hardliner and not a very progressive thinking coach.

2 . **Curly Neal** from **Harlem Globetrotters**. He was maybe the best dribbler ever to play the game. He would often dribble 3-5 balls at one time back in the day during a game and no one else could do it. Everyone saw him as part of the mainstream Globetrotters of the 60's, 70's, and 80's as a circus show but he was indeed good enough to play in the NBA but turned down NBA offers for the money and the fame of the Globetrotters.

3. **Bob Cousey**-maybe the first true point guard of the NBA. He played with the Celtics and won many championships in the 50's and 60's. He only used his right hand most of the time so most don't consider him elite. He often controlled the

game with pace and making sure the right guys had the ball. He was an extension of their head coach the great **Red Aurebach** on the floor.

4-**Allen Iverson** was a shooting guard but dribbled like a point guard. He fortunately or unfortunately changed the game again in the 90's NBA. The social media age and new breed of basketball was now changing to be the street player who was defiant and brash. They now could do things with the ball that most players could not in eras before.

Allen Iverson was around 6-1 if that. But he could dunk despite weighing around only 175 pounds. His speed and quickness was a great asset and he often dribbled out the clock or dribbled the shot clock down to create a hard shot. He even created a few dribble moves in the 90s, one which was a crazy spin dribble that was later banned from the game as a travel or carry violation.

5.	**Steve Nash**-a great dribbler with a great turnover to assist ratio not maybe even matched in today's game. Nash often dribbled left handed more and never looked at the ball. He was often looking up all the time to make the assist. He was not a fancy dribbler but as a coach and teacher of the fundamentals, it's great to see a guy not out there trying to be fancy. His signature move was to dribble behind the basket and come back out on the other side without going out of bounds to find shooters in the corner or passed inside to the big men. He now is an NBA head coach and can coach players to be great guards and good court generals.

6.	**John Stockton** always handled the ball well over his years with the Utah Jazz. Again not a fancy dribbler but never dribbled too much and never turned the ball over despite being small and having a fragile stature. No team could ever make him turn the ball over despite having big guards and wing players guard him in the NBA.

7.	**Rafer Alston**, aka And-1 all star, "Skip To My Loo". He created a move where he skipped with the ball and dribbled that was a cross between a travel and a carry. Sometimes it was called but never in an And-1 game. If you ever want to see some fancy dribble moves, you tube And-1 mixtape DVDs. You'll see some dribble moves that will wow you over.

8- **Kevin Smith** from Ft Worth, TX was the best dribbler I played with at Iowa. He was a year under me and I hosted him on his visit. His girlfriend and my ex-wife were best friends, and roommates for 1 or 2 years in college, and were high school classmates. He had so much quickness and dribbled the ball close to the floor and had all the crossovers and such. But his problem was he had no purpose when he dribbled, he could not get the basket much or beat his man totally. Coach **Davis** didn't like it, that he'd go through his dribble moves and then make the wrong play or pass. Or he would force a contested shot after he dribbled like crazy . He never used his dribble moves to create shots for others and despite us being a team with loaded talent. His assist numbers were very low also compared to other great Iowa guards. Other Iowa Hawkeye guards who played before him or after him didn't have half of his dribble talent skill set.

9-John Wall, Kyrie Irving, and The Professor are all honorable mentions for me in my 2nd edition. John Wall often has the ball on a sting like a magician. Kyrie dribbles like he is in the Matrix. So low and very similar like Kemba Walker both are. But the most entertaining might be The Professor, another And 1 mixtape star. He was a white skinny guard who crossed up a lot of dudes in the parks and was so nice. He now dresses up like superheroes and plays on local courts and embarases dudes.

Here are a few dribble drills I teach kids at camps and training and even my own kids:

1-**Right hand dribble-Dribble** down full court and
right hand back down court
 2-**left hand dribble dribble** down full court and left
hand down back.
3-Right-left alternating- full court dribble using both hands 1 then the
other.
4- Backwards right hand down and
back.
 5-**backwards left hand-** down and
back
6-**backwards right left down** and
back
7-**4 dribbles up and 2 back right**
hand
8- **4 dribbles up and 2 back left**
hand.
9-**mixture dribble- players** go down and back where the player mixes
up their dribble routine on whatever they want to do.
10—**Mixture- dribble backwards** down and back anyway they want to.

All these drills are great for small kids and even older players when done
quickly. They will ensure they will be able to handle the ball equally with
both hands when they are older.

Walk the dog-Right hand rolls ball, left hand dribbles while walking

Coach Earl's Passing

Often an overlooked fundamental of the game as fancy dribblers have now come into play. In the old days of basketball the fast break was true basketball, with the ball never hitting the floor. In the 60-70s passing was stressed as all 5 positions were played by players. Then in the 90s, when dribbling became dominant, passing was put on the back burner.

Here is a list of basic and advance passes each

player should have

A: <u>Basic passes</u>

1 - **Chest pass** - The pass is thrown and caught from chest position. Bobby Knight had all his players execute the perfect chest pass in his offense at Indiana.

2 – **Bounce pass** - The ball is thrown from off your knee in a basketball stance low position. The ball should be bounced a little over half the distance from the other offensive player. When I played for Coach **Davis** at the University of Iowa he taught the bounce pass as a normal pass in our offense. His thought process was that the defense is taught to have their hands up and not hands down. So the bounce pass was harder to defend by active hands defenders.

3-**Overhead pass** – Often used as an outlet pass off the rebound to ignite the fast break. Great centers such as **Bill Walton**, Wes Unseld, **Wilt Chamberlain**, and now **Kevin Love** use the overhead pass. Overhead passes are also used to pass over the zone in the half-court offense.

<u>Advanced passes</u>

1-   **Behind the Back pass-** as used by Pistol Pete Maravich, and other guards such as Jerry West and James Harden.

2-   **One-Hand Bullet** pass-used to zip the ball thru defenders at a high velocity. Also can be a bounce pass as they use the one hand quicker like Magic or Stockton used to do and zip it off the defensive player's ear.

3-   **Thru the Legs pass** -used to pass between the defenders legs when they are in a wide defensive stance. Now called nutmegged lol.

4-   **Off the defenders back, butt or leg pass** - Often used to keep the possession by the offensive player when they take the ball out of under bounds. They often use it on out of bounds plays when the defensive

player has his back turned to them. Or They can throw it off their back or
butt or when the offensive player loses his dribble and no offensive players are
available. The offensive player bounces the ball off the leg of the defender and
then
gets his dribble again to prevent a 5 second violation or turnover. Often called
a smart or heady play.

Some of the best passers I've seen are:

1-Magic Johnson- Maybe the flashiest passer ever to play the game. Magic used a variety of speed and no-look passes to set up his teammates. He is also third all time **NBA** career assist leader despite having his career cut short early.

1-   **Sherman Douglas**-in College he played for Syracuse. He used to throw half court alley hoop passes to **Derrick Coleman** and **Rony Sikley**. I played with **Sherman** while playing with the Celtics and he always made the pass the defense couldn't see.   Even sometimes he would hit you on the back of the head on purpose to teach you never to turn your head away from the ball.

2-   **Pistol Pete Maravich-**Often made flashy bold passes. He would move the ball around his body and then pass to an open teammate. People often called him a hotdog when he played but he was ahead of his time.

3-**John Stockton,**-often made the right pass and not too flashy at the right time.

4-   **Mark Jackson**-he was both flashy and solid and is actually the 2nd leading assist man in NBA history. A great heady guard who played the game in his head and on the floor. Today a great announcer who has a great take on the game.

5-   - **LeBron James, Danny Manning, Vlade Divac, Arvydas Sabonis, Chris Webber**, are others that deserve mention. All were great passers for their position despite being over 6-8 and many 7 feet and above. The way they passed over the defense and saw the defense before it adjusted to them was legendary.

6-   **Ray Thompson**, the best passer I played with at Iowa was from Argo, IL. He was a top 25 H.S. recruit and McDonald's All-American. He was a 6-5 swing guard- forward that played at a high level and had great vision. Ray T averaged 5 assists per game or more during his short career at Iowa.

Dani Lyons 55- Behind the back
pass

<u>**Other Books to Look for from Coach Acie Earl in**</u> Amazon or Itunes etc online.

Slavery In sports -The Role of the Black athlete.

Archie Early-A star is born, read about one of the best players ever to come from a small town in Moline, Illinois.

How to Produce a College Athlete 2nd edition
If your pro player and you have kids, every player thinks their child is going to be as good if not better than you. However stats say their children are often worse than the average child. Read my thoughts on how to produce a college athlete in any sport by personal training.   Speed and agility training, diet, AAU travel team, summer camps and attending the best high school in the area are all things Coach Earl writes about.

How to Play Overseas-31 rules every player should know.
All College/Semi Pro players now have a guide to playing abroad. To make money, and fit in and others in and outs , Coach Earl writes about. Read Coach Earl's 35 chapter -step program that allowed him to play in over 12 Countries in 8 years and earn 3 MVP's awards.

For questions or comments on this book, or to host to a book signing or fund raiser for your school or organization email or call Coach Acie Earl at: 319 430-2537- coachaearl@aol.com

**You can also book Coach Earl
For speaking engagements to
motivate your staff or students.**